REDEFINED

*RECLAIM YOUR POWER
AND LIVE THE LIFE YOU WANT*

LAKEYSHA COBBS-HAYES
MAT, BCBA

Redefined: Reclaim Your Power and Live the Life You Want. Copyright 2024 by Lakeysha Cobbs-Hayes.

All rights reserved. No part of this publication may be reproduced, distributed, or transmitted in any form or by any means, including photocopying, recording, or other electronic or mechanical methods, without the prior written permission of the publisher except in the case of brief quotations embodied in critical reviews and certain other noncommercial uses permitted by copyright law.

For permission requests, write to the publisher addressed "Attention: Permissions Coordinator," 205 N. Michigan Avenue, Suite #810, Chicago, IL 60601. 13th & Joan books may be purchased for educational, business or sales promotional use. For information, please email the Sales Department at sales@13thandjoan.com.

Printed in the U. S. A.

First Printing, January 2025

Library of Congress Cataloging-in-Publication Data has been applied for.

ISBN: 978-1-7322479-6-3

ABOUT THIS BOOK

To Mrs. Brown, my 10th-grade world history teacher and mentor. Thank you for seeing the potential in me before I could see it in myself. Your wisdom, guidance and belief changed the trajectory of my life. I will be forever grateful.

CONTENTS

Preface 1

PART I: REDEFINING YOUR MINDSET 15
Chapter 1: Yes, You Deserve It 17
Chapter 2: Your Life Is Fucked Up? Good. 30
Chapter 3: Radical Honesty 39
Chapter 4: Resistance to Redefining 55
Chapter 5: Resilience 69
Chapter 6: Radical Responsibility 83
Chapter 7: Redefining Your Relationships 98

PART II: REDEFINING YOUR LIFE 129
Chapter 8: The Redefining Process 131

ACKNOWLEDGMENTS

First and foremost, I want to thank God for the strength, resilience, and wisdom to not only survive my story but to thrive in spite of it. Without faith, none of this would be possible.

To my husband, Randall: You are my rock, my best friend, and my biggest supporter. Thank you for loving me through every phase of my journey, for celebrating my wins and for picking me up during my losses. Your unwavering belief in me has been a constant source of strength. I love you more than words can express.

To my children: You are my reasons WHY! Everything I do, I do for you. Thank you for being my greatest teachers, my most honest mirrors, and my most profound motivation. I am so proud to be your mother.

To my siblings: We have been through so much together. Though our paths have been different, our bond is unbreakable. Thank you for being my first friends, my earliest allies, and my constant reminders of where we come from and what we're capable of. I love you all deeply.

To my grandmother, my angel: Though you are no longer with us, your love and guidance continue to shape my life. Thank you for being the first person to see beyond my circumstances and believe in my potential. I carry you with me always.

To Mrs. Brown, my 10th-grade world history teacher: You changed the trajectory of my life with your simple daily question, "Are you coming back tomorrow?" Thank you for seeing me, for believing in me, and for planting the seeds of possibility that would eventually bloom into the life I have today.

To my Key Essentials to Behavior Management, Corp family: I am so grateful for your dedication, your hard work, and your shared commitment to our mission. Thank you for being part of this dream and for helping me to build something bigger than myself.

To my clients and mentees: Thank you for trusting me with your stories, your struggles, and your triumphs. It is an honor to witness your transformation and to play a role in your journey. You inspire me every day.

To my friends: Thank you for being my chosen family, my laughter, and my safe space. Your love and support mean the world to me.

To Lynda, my chief of operations: Your partnership and friendship have been instrumental in the growth of Key Essentials and in my own personal growth. Thank you for being my sounding board, my problem-solver, and my right hand.

A special thank you to Stephanie Manns: Thank you for your incredible talent, your patience, and your dedication in helping me bring my story and my message to life on these pages. Your ability to capture my voice and my heart has been a true gift. This book wouldn't be what it is without you.

And finally, to you, the reader: Thank you for holding this book in your hands. Thank you for being open to the message and the journey within these pages. My deepest hope is that this book will spark something within you: A remembering of your own power, a reclaiming of your own story. You are the reason I wrote this book. You are the reason I do this work. You are the reason I believe in redefinition.

We are in this together. Let's redefine what's possible.

With lots of love and gratitude,
Keysha

*The only way to deal with an unfree world
is to become so absolutely free
that your very existence is an act of rebellion.*

Albert Camus

re·de·fined
/ˌrēdəˈfīned/
verb
The result of putting in the work to become whatever the f@#k you want.

PREFACE

"**A**RE YOU COMING BACK TOMORROW?"
That was the question that my 10th-grade world history teacher, Mrs. Brown, asked me every day that school year. In a building full of thousands of kids, I didn't understand why she was so interested in what I was or wasn't doing, particularly since I was doing everything I could not be noticed. Wearing hospital-style, no-slip socks as shoes with a slicked-back ponytail and a slick mouth to match, I didn't care about shit—including myself—and it showed. My angry, fuck-all-these-rules demeanor was a cover-up for resentment, disappointment, and sadness—the damage that years of abuse and abandonment had left behind.

At that point, school had become completely optional for me. I was ditching class a lot. School was mostly a place I went to pass the time. My foster mother wouldn't allow anybody to be in her house until after 5:30 p.m. when she came home from work. With nowhere else to go, school was where I went to hang out with my friends and maybe sit in a class or two, like Mrs. Brown's, out of boredom.

In the afternoons, she ate her lunch in her classroom with two other teachers, Ms. Little and Ms. Mathis. Mrs. Brown had an open-door policy and would let students come in too. For 30 minutes, my friends and I would chill, talking to the teachers and wilding out. Once I figured out that my wild antics, trash-talking, and dry sense of humor made the teachers laugh, lunch in Mrs. Brown's class became my own show.

The beauty about Mrs. Brown was she let me be who I was. Eventually, I'd get that she saw the potential in me that I hadn't yet, but she never scolded me for acting a fool or pressured me to do anything different. I didn't realize then that she'd noticed me skipping school and aimlessly hanging around the building in the afternoons.

So her asking me if I was coming back to her class the following day was her way of gently acknowledging that she saw me in many ways while subtly reminding me that I had somewhere I should be. Something about me stood out to Mrs. Brown, and it was more than the socks that I wore in the hallways. She made me feel like she looked forward to seeing me every day. There was a part of me that looked forward to seeing her too.

Yet every time Mrs. Brown would yell out, "Are you coming back tomorrow?" as I got to the door of her classroom, it annoyed me.

I'd think to myself, *Why the hell does this woman keep asking me that?*

I wasn't used to an adult caring about my whereabouts, and I certainly wasn't used to being given a choice about anything.

Require me to do something? Definitely. Expect me to do something? Yes. Give me an option? Absolutely not.

Adults in my life, until I met Mrs. Brown, didn't make me feel like I had a say about anything that happened to me. But as our relationship grew, Mrs. Brown was the first person to teach me about the power of choice. She reminded me that I had a choice about coming back to school. She challenged me to see that while I could be so much more, I didn't have to change my life if I didn't want to. She taught me that my life was a direct result of what I decided to do with it every day.

Her daily question held me accountable—at first to her and eventually to myself.

PREFACE

Mrs. Brown was more than a teacher. She was a God-sent mentor who became a mirror to show me who I could be. But it was up to me to become her.

If I told you everything that has happened to me in my life (a lot of which I'll share in this book), you would wonder how it's possible to be who I am and to have done what I've done.

I am nothing that I am supposed to be. I was raised by a dysfunctional mother who never believed me or believed in me. The man who I knew to be my father died in prison. After being sexually abused, I was taken from my mother and put in foster care. I barely graduated from high school with straight Ds. And I had six children by the time I was 28 years old.

But I've also built a multi-million-dollar, multi-location behavioral health practice that supports hundreds of families across southern California. I teach and train all over the country. I live in a home that I love, and I have a beautiful family and life with my husband and children. I am someone people can count on—including myself.

And I am living proof that you get to decide how life goes for you. You get to choose who you want to be.

So today I am here to be for you what Mrs. Brown was for me. I am here to be your teacher, your mentor, your messenger, and your mirror. I am here to remind you that you too have a choice about what happens to you from here on out.

I am here to ask you: "Are you coming back?"

Are you coming back to the you who you are still supposed to become despite everything that's happened to you?

Are you coming back to the person you were on the path to becoming before you got hurt?

Are you coming back to who you were before somebody told you that you wouldn't be shit—and you believed them?

Are you coming back for the success you saw before that one failure or mistake scared you so much that you stopped trying?

Are you coming back to the version of you that you *want* to be instead of who you *should* be?

I hope so.

WHY I WROTE THIS BOOK FOR YOU

If you picked up this book, there is a strong chance that there is something about yourself or your life that you deeply desire to change. In fact, there may be a lot of things about yourself or your life that you want to change. If that's true, you are in the right place at the right time with the right guide and the right book.

In these pages, I'll teach you how to unlearn some old beliefs and behaviors, learn some new ones, and apply what you learn to drastically improve your life.

But if I had to sum up why you've holding this book in your hands, it all comes down to this:

I wrote this book to help you push past the shit that is keeping you from changing what you want to change and becoming who you want to be.

I wrote this book because I've been you. I've been the teenager who knew that her life could be so much better but had no idea how to recreate her reality and get from where she was to where she wanted to be. I've also been the very grown adult who achieved the better life that her younger self felt was so out of reach, the woman who achieved more than she could have ever imagined.

I've been homeless and hopeless. I've had as many setbacks as I've had comebacks.

I've lived through trauma that no child should ever experience. I've had things happen to me that should have stretched me out on the floor (physically and emotionally), so much so that people who know me couldn't believe that I was still going.

But I did keep going – just like you did.

With everything that's happened to me, I could have easily given up. Checked out. Accepted a minimum and mediocre life that barely scratched the surface of what the world has for me. Instead, I decided that I still had a life to live and people to take care of, most importantly myself.

I still deserved to try. I still deserved a shot. I still deserved a chance to live. And eventually, that desire to live became the declaration that I deserved the best damn life that I could possibly have. I didn't want to survive. I wanted to thrive.

This book is my chance to put exactly how I did it on paper so that you can do it too. I opened this book by sharing a story about one of the most influential people in my life, Mrs. Brown, one of my high school teachers.

Until she came into my life, I didn't know what it felt like to have someone believe in me. Mrs. Brown empowered me to see myself, my life, and my possibility and potential differently. And she also helped me to see other people differently too—specifically people who came into my life to help me.

I am far from a religious person and while I can't quote the Bible backward and forwards, I do believe in the power of something bigger than us. I believe that meeting Mrs. Brown supernaturally set something in motion in my life that hasn't stopped since then.

Support shows up for me.

Whenever I am in the midst of a major growth spurt in my life and expanding myself in some way, someone shows up. In most instances, it's someone who I don't know, but who holds the keys to some information that I need to take my next steps.

From guiding me toward the life-defining decision to choose early childhood education as my college major—if you'd met me then, you would understand that I never saw myself sitting in a college classroom, much less working with children for a living—to acquiring a lease for a sensory gym that I had no plan to purchase but has made me hundreds of thousands of dollars, help has come. Every time, those people appeared and saw fit to help me. They said the right thing at the right time. They became my compass and pointed me in the right direction.

It may have been a big idea or a small step that would ultimately lead me to something much bigger but in either case, I acted on it. I moved, even when I didn't know what I was doing. I saw the full picture. I was scared, but I listened. I took the action. I did the work. I needed help, and it came in the form of someone who I didn't know and who, until then, didn't know me.

I say all of that to say this: If you're still reading this, that means something. Do you know what that is?

Support is showing up for you.

Don't miss this moment— *your* moment. This is your moment to finally get it, to break through and to break free. The moment when you decide, once and for all, to change. To finally fix "it," whatever your "it" is. The moment to reclaim what belongs to you. Yourself. Your stuff. Your success. *All of it.* This is your defining moment to redefine yourself and your life.

This is the moment and someone has shown up for *you*.

Regardless of what your family or friend circle looks like right now, you have somebody in this world who believes in you. And that person is me. Give me a little bit of time and I'll change your mind. If I can change your mind, I can change your life.

If you've ever felt it before, you know that when someone believes in you, it's a powerful thing. Belief sparks something in us. It lights a fire. Belief can be the motivation you need to begin, to begin again— and ultimately, to win.

Yes, having someone believe in you is an amazing thing. But do you know what's even more beautiful than someone else believing in you?

Believing in yourself.
Without that, nothing else matters.

If you live on this planet, chances are you know Oprah Winfrey. One of the wealthiest women in the world and arguably the Queen of Personal Transformation, she has said this: "You don't become what you want. You become what you believe."

Yet again, Oprah, you've given us words to live by. And those are words that I want to tattoo on your eyelids so you can see them when you sleep.

It's easy to look at Oprah now and think that she has an extraordinary life. It's true, she undeniably does. But there was nothing about how her life started—abandoned by her biological mother, sexually abused as a little girl, pregnant as a teenager—that would have given any indication that she would become who she is today. She completely transformed herself. She put in the work to master her mind, her craft, and her life. She redefined herself and her life.

She believed, and so she became.

You may not want to own your own media empire or start a girls' school in South Africa like Oprah has, but you have something you want to achieve in this life.

Wanting to be different is not enough. You have to believe it.

I'm not going to sugarcoat this for you at all—I'm going to ask a lot of you. Redefining yourself is messy as hell, and I am not here to convince you that it's not. This will be hard work, probably the hardest work you've ever done. None of it is even possible if you don't believe in yourself. Like all the other work that you will need to do to change your life, self-belief is something that no one else can do for you but you.

Believe in your ability to change and to become better.

Believe in your ability to learn. Believe that you can have, do, and be more, whatever that looks like for you. Believe that it gets to be better.

If you can believe and change your behaviors to align with that belief, anything is possible.

Anything.

WHO THIS BOOK IS FOR...

This book is for people who want to change something about themselves and their lives. It could be to lose weight or add income to your bank account. It doesn't matter. There is something about your life that you want to be different, something you *need* to be different. But you haven't been able to get from where you are to where you want to be.

You've spent so much time wondering why you can't get it right. You've been beating your head against the wall because you can't figure it out. You don't understand why life is so hard for you.

So how is that showing up in your life? Let me guess:

- **You've secretly lost hope that anything will ever be different. (It's okay, you're human.).** Whether you can't catch a break and life keeps hitting you hard no matter how hard you try, or you keep making the same mistakes over and over again, the constant disappointment has you down. You listen to all the motivational podcasts, make all the plans, and say all the prayers but deep down, you really don't believe you can have a different life.
- **You secretly hate your life.** You don't love your life—you're just living it. You are showing up at work, in school, doing the things that you should be doing, and going through the motions. It could be a good life, great even, but it's not good or great for *you* anymore. For you, this life is mediocre at

best. You know you are meant for more, but you have no idea where to start. You feel torn between who you are and who you want to be.

- **You keep messing up.** You're constantly taking two steps forward toward a positive path in your life. But every time you make a little progress, you somehow find yourself taking 10 steps back. You've tried to create positive change in your life, and you've failed. Many times.
- **Your life is so fucked up that you're doing nothing.** Maybe your past trauma or present circumstances have you so paralyzed by fear that you haven't moved at all, at least not in a *really* long time.

Any of this feel familiar? I figured as much. Well, the good news is that help is here. This book is for you.

Keep reading.

…AND WHO THIS BOOK IS NOT FOR

Since you're still hanging in there with me and we're just getting to know each other, I feel compelled to set some things straight before we move any further.

You may be standing at the shelf in a bookstore flipping through this book or reading a sample on your Kindle right now thinking to yourself, "I may have just met the woman of my dreams." Maybe you're ready to give me your money and buy the book. I thank you for your support. Before you run to the register or hit that "Buy Now" button, let me give you some more truth:

This book is not for the faint at heart—and neither am I.

In case you haven't figured it out yet, I am a straight shooter. I don't beat around the bush, and I don't do a lot of fluff-filled conversations. I am as direct as they come. I love helping people get to a win, but I am very much a call-you-to-the-carpet, call-you-out-on-your-shit type of coach. I believe that I worked for mine, so you should work for yours.

So I am not the coach and this is not the book for you if—

- **You're looking for someone to allow you to feel sorry for yourself.** Life is hard for every last one of us. Bad things have happened and will continue to happen as long as we're alive. We have to keep moving. If you want to wallow and not work, you should keep moving too.
- **You're committed to bullshit excuses.** There's a motivational speaker, Trevor Otts, who says, "If you want to fight for your limitations, you get to keep them." I'm going to leave it at that.
- **You're content with your life as is.** If you're here, this is unlikely the case, but that doesn't mean that your life feels so itchy to you that you're willing to change it. If you dislike changing more than your current situation, then you are welcome to stay there.

Listen, I get you. I understand exactly where you are and why you are. And that's why I am not going to go easy on you.

It's very appropriate that this is a self-help book because that is exactly what I am here to help you do—help yourself. Sometimes support comes into your life for a long time. Sometimes it's just long enough to drop a nugget of information on you or point you in the right direction, and it's then up to you to take your ball and run with it.

I am here to alleviate the excuse of you not knowing what to do. By the end of this book, you will know what to do. But what I can't do is do it for you.

Yes, I am an advocate for coaching, mentoring, and surrounding yourself with people who educate, empower, and encourage you. People who love on you, support you, and celebrate you. You deserve that.

PREFACE

But people can't replace your part of the process. The only one who can do the real work, *your work*, is you. No one—not someone who loves you deeply or even the best, most motivational coach—can do it for you. They can't hold your hand the entire way. They can't keep you from failing or falling. Yes, that's part of the process, too.

This is *your* life.

Work it or don't. It's up to you.

WARNING: THIS MAY HURT A LITTLE. (OKAY, A LOT.)

One summer, I was on vacation with a group of family and friends.

We were all having a great time, chilling in the sun, drinking and eating a little too much, you know, overindulging and doing what people who escape their lives for a week tend to do.

The conversation was great—until it wasn't.

Somehow we got on the topic of someone who I didn't know, but someone else in the group did, who had recently hit a rough patch in life.

The guy who was sharing the story with us went on and on about the situation, adding in repeatedly how bad he felt for the person who was struggling.

I listened patiently—at least patiently for me, which was probably about 10 seconds—until finally, I couldn't take it anymore.

Turning to him, I asked, "Do you really feel *that* bad?"

You would have thought somebody pulled the plug from the DJ's turntable at the house party, and the music suddenly stopped. Shocked, everyone shut down immediately.

I could see steam coming from the top of Mr. Storyteller's head. He was hot and ready to challenge me.

"What?," he said.

If he thought I was going to back down, clearly he didn't know me that well. Putting on my no-nonsense tone coupled with my clinical behavioral therapist hat, I doubled down.

"I said, 'Do you really feel that bad?' Because if you did, you would do something about it. You don't feel bad. You may empathize. You may even have sympathy for them. But if you felt that bad, you would do something about it. You don't feel bad enough."

The truth hurts, doesn't it?

How often have we been that guy? How often do we sit around and talk about how horrible we feel about something we see happening to somebody else, trying to convince ourselves and maybe others that we would do something if we could? Well, guess what?

If we wanted to, we would.

Would you watch a kid get pummeled in the street and not do anything? Would you let someone pull out a gun on somebody you love and not move? Likely, the answer is "No." You wouldn't. Why? Because you care. Because it's important to you. So important that you are instinctively motivated to move, to do whatever you have to do to save that person from being hurt. It's an inner pull, a will that tells your brain, "I have to do something about this." And when that turns on, there is nothing that can be done to stop it.

Ready for another truth bomb?

This doesn't just apply when it comes to people we care about. It applies to us too.

Here's the fact: If you really wanted your life to change, you would have done it by now.

Let's talk about what is standing in the way between you and the will you need to really do something about your life:

- **You're sitting in shit and trying to turn it into sunshine.** You know there's better. But it's far easier to sit, settle, and hope for something to change than to do something about it. So you don't.

- **You don't have a system set up for success.** It's not enough to change yourself. You have to change everything around you. Have you ever tried not to eat ice cream with a freezer full of ice cream? Have you ever tried to run on the treadmill in high heels? Tried to transform your mindset without a coach and a counselor or therapist? And how's that working for you?
- **You don't really believe you can do it.** Yep, back to the belief. You will only go as far as your belief in yourself.
- **You haven't been willing to work for it.** I know you're thinking, "Here she goes with that again!" You're right. I can't say it enough. No work. No results. No change. It's that simple.

The bottom line is this: Until your life feels so unbearable, you will not change it.

As a professional behavioral therapist who has practiced for more than 20 years, I meet people almost every day who need to change something about themselves. From preteens to people well into their 40s, some patients, some staff, and some friends who I just care about personally, they all have one thing in common: They're struggling in some aspect of their life, and they're stuck.

While some of them are living with mental health disorders such as anxiety, autism, or ADHD that can make their day-to-day lives and changes challenging, where there is a will, there is a way.

Those who are willing to change do with my help and the right tools and treatment plans.

The secret to their success?: **Beliefs and behaviors.**

If you can master both, you can master your life.

This book will teach you how.

Part I

REDEFINING YOUR MINDSET

1

YES, YOU DESERVE IT

IMAGINE THIS.

You're hungry. *Actually, you're starving.*

You have time to cook, but instead of going into the kitchen and cooking a healthy-ish meal with the groceries that you lugged from the car to the kitchen yesterday (not to mention paid for with your hard-earned money), you decide that skinless chicken breast and broccoli isn't going to cut it. You've worked your ass off all day, the world has worked your last nerve, and so you deserve to treat yourself. You *need* to treat yourself. And there is only one thing that will do. You grab your keys and wallet, and you're out.

Drive-thru, here I come.

A few minutes later, you pull off from the pick-up window with that paper bag propped up on the passenger seat and as soon as you take your first bite, it's clear that the Grease Gods are shining their light on you. Your large fries are perfectly salty and piping hot. Your burger is grilled to perfection, and your Coke is crispy and ice cold.

Now, this is a dinner, you think to yourself. In your mind, you're set for the night.

Until an hour or two later when your stomach has the audacity to let you know that you're starving—again. You may remember that 3,000 calories of fatty flavor that you inhaled in the five miles between your house and your favorite fast-food spot but for your belly, that is all in the past. It wants food. *Now.*

No amount of processed food is going to give your body the satisfaction it's looking for or needs.

This friends, is the same sensation you're having when it comes to your self-esteem and your sense of worthiness.

You can eat, or in this case achieve, a truckload of good things. None of it feels good to you long-term because you don't believe you deserve it. No matter how many great things you do, how great other people tell you that you are—hell, how great you *know* you are—it all feels like empty calories, a bottomless pit, and you're never full. You can't wrap your mind around the fact that, yes, you are as amazing as your resume, relationships, revenue, or salary say you are. Or perhaps, if you are in the process of turning your life around, as amazing as any or all of those things will be in your not-so-far-off future. You're waiting to feel worthy but for some reason, you can't.

Cue The Ghetto Boyz's "Mind Playing Tricks on Me" because that is exactly what's happening.

Your mind is so used to filling up on negativity and counting on you losing in life that it doesn't know how to recognize when you're winning.

So, what does it do? Try to convince you that it's all lies. That you can't possibly have achieved this. That at some point, someone is going to find out that you're a fraud or how many times you've really fucked up and come to snatch all your success from you. That you don't know as much as you think you do, so failure is inevitable. That you may have been able to get this far, but there is no way you could go further. That you can't have the love, looks, or life that you want, regardless of what your reality is showing you.

It's all lies.

The truth?

Your mind would rather hold on to the made-up story that you aren't shit than believe the facts that say otherwise.

So, you have to change it. Change your mind, change your life.

If you want to redefine, you have to master your mind so that you can move forward with your life and create a new version of yourself.

Believe it or not, the lies that your mind is holding on to, all of which are creating your lack of worthiness, are not your fault. When your sense of worthiness, security, and adequacy have been torn down over and over and no one has ever built you up and believed in you, it's almost impossible to believe in yourself.

The ugly word from your parents or families or teachers or punk-ass kids in the neighborhood became your truth.

Or growing up, everywhere you looked, there was nothing that reflected anything positive. You lived and went to school in the hood, and people who come from where you come from aren't supposed to make it. The color of your skin, your gender, your grades, none of it pointed to possibility.

You can stop beating yourself up for not knowing how to believe in yourself or that you deserve to have what you have or what you want.

Unworthiness is one of those sneaky feelings, so sneaky that you may not realize that you're struggling with it. If you've been reading this thinking how much everything I've said so far in this chapter is *not* you, not so fast.

Let's look at some of the ways that unworthiness may be sneaking up into your life:

- **You talk yourself out of success.** Whenever you have a shot at doing something that stretches you, you find every reason imaginable why you can't or shouldn't go for it. You ask, work, and pray for something and when it shows up, you get scared. Someone could be handing you your ideal life on a silver platter and as much as you want to reach out your hands to grab it, you can't.
- **You settle.** Everything is telling you that it's wrong. The job. The client. The relationship. You know that it/they are no good for you but over time, you've convinced yourself that you can't have better.
- **You run and hide whenever something bad happens.** To live is to be rejected or to fail. It happens. But for you, it's the train stop where you always get off.
- **You want to run and hide even when something bad could happen but hasn't happened yet.** Instead of living your life on offense, you prefer the proactive approach. You're so convinced that life is going to do you dirty and not work out that any situation that smells like it could hurt you or not work out exactly like you'd like feels like too much risk. You get rid of it before it can get rid of you.
- **You find a way to fuck up when things are going for you. Therapists call it self-sabotaging.** Finally, things are moving in the right direction. The exercise and saying no to those late-night chips are paying off and you're losing the weight, but as soon as you see the scale move, you suddenly have an irresistible urge to eat everything in sight. After all those heartbreaks and being treated like trash for years, you find a partner who worships the ground you walk on. You repay them by constantly picking stupid fights until they give up and leave. You feel uncomfortable with anything good happening to you or for you.

And then there is the sneaky way that unworthiness shows up for a lot of us, including me: Constantly questioning if you really deserve it.

This whole living your dream thing is a lot harder than it sounds. I have a great life, one that I've worked my ass off to have, but there are times when I still feel like the little girl who just wanted to know that she could. Even after all that I've achieved, I still struggle with insecurities. I wonder if I'm enough and if what got me here can get me there, to where I see my life and business going next.

I have people depending on me. A whole ass family including a grandbaby, a whole ass team, a whole ass roster of clients, business partners, mentors...the list goes on and on.

All these people are looking at me and up to me, not for my beauty but for answers. They are expecting me to solve their problems, to lead, guide, and provide for them, to tell them that it's going to be okay when their world is falling apart.

They look at me and see Superwoman. And sometimes, most of the time, I do too. But there are days when I look at myself and still see a rowdy, rough-around-the-edges 26-year-old chick from Southern California with six kids who only graduated from high school because somebody with some sense saw more for her than she could see for herself.

Society and statistics never told me that someone like me could do what I've done. I didn't have examples at home or anywhere around me. According to what most of my world predicted and what I believed about myself, I should be living in the projects, broke and broken, waiting for my food stamps to feed my kids, not building companies or boarding flights to vacation wherever I want to go whenever I want to go there. I spent years doubting myself, even though I was putting one foot in front of the other, doing the work, making better decisions, falling, and getting back up, and I had the success to prove it.

As I've waged my own war against insecurity, self-doubt, and unworthiness, you name an emotion, and I've experienced it.

I've unintentionally self-sabotaged my success, and I've also made my share of dumbass decisions that at the time, I knew with everything in me would end up horribly, but I proceeded without caution and paid for it.

I've been great at adulting and accepting accountability but, unlike Michael Jackson advises in his hit song, I didn't look at the woman in the mirror. I've blamed everyone else when things went wrong.

I've felt proud and patted myself on the back when my hard work resulted in a win, and I've felt so uncomfortable with my success that I've constantly questioned if I deserved it, despite the degrees and million-dollar deposits in my business bank account.

At the root of every dip in this emotional roller coaster has been my feeling unworthy. Now thanks to counseling; constant self-coaching and investing in people to coach and help me when I was in over my head; and learning how to replace negative thoughts, self-talk, beliefs, and behaviors with positive ones; I get them before they get me. I've taught myself how to take big risks, even when something feels a little too scary, and I want to stop. I don't if I believe that the chance I am about to take will make me better in some way. I can sit in the good things that happen to me and tell myself that I deserve it—and believe it.

This is what mind mastery looks like: Staying on high alert and learning how to course correct so you check yourself before you wreck yourself.

YOUR MIND IS LIKE A RADIO STATION. YOU CAN CHANGE IT.

Have you ever taken a road trip and listened to the radio while you were driving? I know I am talking to a playlist and Bluetooth crowd here, but work with me, okay? You're cruising and grooving to a song that you haven't heard in years and just when you start to really get into it, singing off-key at the top of your lungs and all, the song goes to static and you lose it.

You wouldn't sit there and listen to those scratchy noises or the voice of your favorite singer going in and out as you try to catch every other word. You'd flip that knob or keep pressing the hell out of that up arrow until you get to a clear channel again.

It could be static or some trash trap music that you don't want your kids to know you know the words to even though you do and so do they. The point is, if you don't like the channel, you change it.

Start to think about your mind like that radio. When something comes into it that you don't like, change the station. When the greatest hits of your past life pop up like, "I Don't Deserve This," "I Shouldn't Have This!," "This is Too Good For Me," or "I Can't Do This," it's your job to fill your mind and your ears with something different, something better. Make a new playlist, one that is worthy of a worthy person. The new soundtrack of your life should sound much different than the one you're used to hearing.

Instead of the trash that you've been listening to, try some new songs like, "I Get To Have This," "I Believe in Myself," "I Deserve Every Good Thing in My Life," "I'm Not Who They Said I Was," and "I'm Better Now."

Doesn't that sound better?

Now I have to warn you. You'll put down this book feeling full of fire and confidence, ready to conquer your mind and beat down any negativity that comes your way. And then, like that toxic ex who seems to be able to smell your happiness and peace from a hundred miles away, the doubt will try to creep back in. Your mind will want to keep you stuck on the same, tired station. Old habits and thoughts are hard to break. We'll dig into why this happens and what to do about it much more throughout this book but for now, when your mind wants to pull you into negativity and talk you out of moving in a different, more positive direction, put these tips into practice:

- **Stop blaming yourself for not knowing what you didn't know or what you couldn't do.** All of this is new to you. Until now, you didn't have the knowledge, tools, or support to become different or to sustain the change that you've tried to make in the past. Forgive yourself. In the words of Auntie Maya Angelou, "When you know better, you do better."
- **Recognize that it's BS.** When negative thoughts do pop up, don't let them win. Remember, these feelings have been deeply ingrained in you and internalized over time. It takes time to learn new truths. Trust what you can see over what you feel or hear internally and sometimes externally, if you have haters around you. You are changing. You are winning. Don't work overtime to convince yourself that you're not. And for your success's sake, don't believe anyone who tries to come along to tear you down or take you back as you're pushing forward.
- **Don't question yourself too much.** Your mind will try to tell you that if it looks too good to be true, it is. When that happens, understand that when life has been rough for you, everything seems too good to be true. So don't question and doubt yourself out of good things. Rewrite that fear-based statement to this: If it looks too good to be true, it isn't. *It is true. True for me.*

THE LOAD GETS LIGHTER

I wish I could tell you that once you've mastered this mindset thing once, it goes away forever.

It doesn't.

You could be someone who can throw negative thoughts in a mental cell and throw away the key. But for most people, it isn't that simple.

Unworthiness is something that you continue to carry with you. Whenever you are growing, elevating, and expanding yourself, it will sneak in, whispering in your ear, trying to convince you that you're not where you're supposed to be. If you refuse to listen, those nasty, negative thoughts will turn up the volume. But over time, with awareness and intentionally changing how you think about yourself and what you do when negative thoughts and behaviors try to resurface, you bring less and less of that baggage along for the ride.

It's like luggage. You go from needing a full set of bags to carry all your insecurities, self-doubt, and self-sabotage. As you do more work to overwrite those beliefs and behaviors, you'll be able to pack your negativity into a single suitcase. Give it more time and work on yourself, and that big suitcase will become a carry-on.

Before you know it, you've become so good at shifting your mindset that what used to be able to destroy you is now some residual noise in the back of your mind that could fit into a wallet.

The load gets lighter, trust me.

And let me also say this: Questioning yourself doesn't mean that something is wrong with you. You wouldn't be a living, breathing person if you never looked the mountain of fear in the face and wondered if you had what it took to climb it. Some self-doubt or feeling insecure is normal. In fact, it's humbling. And it's human.

When you question yourself, it also doesn't mean that all the work you've done and are doing to master your mind isn't working. Believe that the work is working.

When you get to a point where you can recognize the sound of self-doubt and stop yourself from self-sabotaging, the work is working.

When you can snap yourself back into truth before you derail everything you've worked so hard for and do major damage to yourself, the work is working.

When you receive the rewards of your effort to change yourself and your life, the work is working.

All you have to do is keep working. Keep releasing. Keep redefining.

SHAKE OFF SHAME

Shame is sneaky. We don't recognize it or see it when it shows up.

Sometimes despite how our lives look or how we're showing up in the world, deep down, we don't feel good about ourselves. And our choices tell on us.

Self-sabotage. Destructive patterns. Quitting too early. Picking the wrong people to be in our lives.

All of those are signs that you are struggling with your sense of self-worth, stopping yourself from having the good that you want and deserve because you don't believe you should have it.

Shame is a story that makes you feel minimal, broken, and undeserving. Regardless of what has happened to you or what you've done, you are not damaged goods. You're still good. You still deserve the life you want. You can't let the bad things that have happened to you stop you from having the life you really want.

Shake that shame up off of you.

Now let's talk about those sneaky little things called limiting beliefs. You know those negative, false, or straight-up self-defeating thoughts that creep into your mind and hold you back from living your best life. Yeah, those.

Limiting beliefs are like that toxic friend who always tells you that you can't do something, that you're not good enough, or that you don't deserve happiness. They're the nagging voice in your head that says, "Who do you think you are? You can't achieve that goal!" or "Don't even bother trying something new, people will just judge you."

But here's the thing: Those beliefs are often irrational and not based on any real evidence. They're just overgeneralized assumptions that prevent you from seeing opportunities, taking risks, and reaching for the stars. They keep you stuck in negative patterns and can seriously mess with your self-esteem and overall well-being.

Some common limiting beliefs that might sound familiar:

- "I'm just not good enough."
- "I don't deserve success or happiness."
- "I'll never be able to achieve my dreams."
- "People will judge me if I step out of my comfort zone."
- "I can't trust anyone."

Sound like something that's been playing on repeat in your mind? Well, it's time to change the station!

Recognizing and challenging these limiting beliefs is crucial for your personal growth and self-improvement. You've got to identify these beliefs, question whether they're really true (spoiler alert: they're not), and replace them with empowering and realistic thoughts that lift you up instead of holding you back.

It's time to break free from those self-imposed limitations and unlock your true potential. You are worthy, capable, and deserving of everything you desire. Don't let those limiting beliefs convince you otherwise.

So the next time that negative self-talk starts creeping in, I want you to stop, check yourself, and replace it with an empowering truth. You've got this. Let's shake off those limiting beliefs and start redefining what's possible for your life!

CHAPTER ONE SELF-ASSESSMENT: REDEFINING YOUR WORTH

Alright, let's get real with ourselves for a minute. It's time to take a good, hard look at how we're doing on this journey of redefining our self-worth. So grab a pen, and let's dive into this self-assessment. Remember, this isn't about perfection. It's about progress. Every step forward counts, no matter how small it might seem.

1. Your Surroundings:

- Is there anyone or anything around you that makes you feel like you're not enough?
- What can you do to create a space that lifts you up and reminds you of how amazing you are?

2. Your Actions:

- Do you ever catch yourself self-sabotaging when things are going well?
- Are you settling for less than you deserve in any area of your life, such as relationships or your career?
- What actions can you take to show yourself some love and remind yourself of your worth?

3. Your Skills:

- What new skills or knowledge can you pick up to help you kick those limiting beliefs to the curb and boost your confidence?
- How can you get better at catching and shutting down that negative self-talk when it pops up?

4. Your Beliefs:

- What are those limiting beliefs you're holding on to about yourself and what you deserve?
- How can you flip the script and start believing in the truth of your inherent worth?
- What values and beliefs do you want to embrace to support your growth and self-esteem?

5. Who You Are:

- How do you define yourself right now, and is that definition really showing off all your potential?
- What qualities do you want to embody as you redefine who you are?
- How can you cultivate an identity that's rooted in your true worth and limitless potential?

6. Your Purpose:

- What's the bigger picture behind why you want to redefine your self-worth?
- How can you trust your gut and have faith in this journey of transformation?
- As you grow in self-love and acceptance, how do you want to make a difference in the world?

Take a minute to look over your answers and see if anything jumps out at you. What steps can you take to work on each area and keep moving forward on this journey? And remember, be kind to yourself. Celebrate your wins, no matter how big or small.

Now let's create an affirmation that resonates with you and supports your growth. Here's an example: "I am worthy and deserving of love, respect, and abundance. I choose to embrace my true potential and create a life that reflects my deepest values."

Repeat that affirmation to yourself daily, and let it sink in. You've got this. Keep doing the work, keep redefining your worth, and watch as your life transforms before your eyes.

2

YOUR LIFE IS FUCKED UP? GOOD.

There is something about your life that you hate. I know that hate is a harsh word, and it's meant to be because that is how you need to feel about your life and current situation to do anything about it.

You cannot change from a space of comfort. For you to do what it takes to change your life, you have to be extremely uncomfortable. Not that half-hearted, this-sucks-but-I-can-live-with-it, in-and-out commitment mindset and behavior that you're used to. That is not going to work.

You have to hate something about your life. You have to be completely fed up and tired of something to change it. You have to be tired of sitting in your own shit and smelling yourself. You have to feel like it is impossible for you to go on one more day, living the way you're living and feeling how you're feeling right now. You have to have had enough.

Until you are at *that* point, the point where you can't take it (or fake it) anymore, the point where you will do anything necessary to change, the point where you feel like this *has* to happen, you don't want it bad enough.

And honestly, you should stop reading this book right now and come back to it when you are ready.

I hope you keep reading. But in case you are on the fence about continuing, I want you to do this first: Imagine that you take the path of least resistance and you give up. You stop here. No more awareness about yourself and who you are. No more learning about how to change your life. No more stretching yourself beyond what you thought you were capable of. And that leaves you continuing the path that you're on now.

Imagine yourself 10, 20, 30 years ahead, and you're still right here in this space. Stuck. Struggling. Unhappy. Overweight. Broke. Frustrated. Sad. Angry.

Maybe you know that your life needs to change and that you're not where you want to be, but you can't quite sum it up into one word. There are signs that you're not living the life you want. Let's see if these feel familiar:

It doesn't feel good. On most days, you feel like you are in agony. This is not the life you want. It's not what you want to do. You're going with the flow of your life, but you're frustrated. You know there is more available to you out there, but you can't have it.

You feel out of place. You're disconnected from the life and identity that you've created.

You're showing up and doing what needs to be done, but you feel like a fake doing it.

You know you're not living your truth.

Your life feels like a lie. As hard as you're trying to be who you think you're supposed to be, it constantly backfires on you, and you explode. You love your kids but you need space, so why are you a stay-at-home mom? You have a customer service job but you hate people?

You say you want to lose weight and are in the gym with a trainer five days a week, but you're home eating doughnuts? You keep trying, but you can't hold the role you're trying so hard to play.

You're living the life "they" want you to live. You are the person you think other people want you to be. You've become what you've seen, what you've been taught and told, be it by your parents or some self-help guru.

You're not calling the shots in your life. Instead, you're just accepting what comes. You're living this by-default life and not taking control over what is happening to and for you. You're allowing external forces—your circumstances, the chatter from other people's opinions—to make internal decisions by not choosing for yourself. You're living the life that you've been given and not the life you want.

You push people away. Living a lie will make you frustrated and angry. You're mad at life. You're defensive and argumentative. You show your true colors, and you're not able to maintain or keep friends. You can't communicate with others. Your unhappiness is constantly boiling over, and you can't help but project it onto others. It feels easier to be alone.

You're constantly complaining. You hate getting up every day, and you're living an "I Gotta Life…" You know the one: I gotta get up. I gotta go to work. I gotta do this, and I gotta do that. You feel trapped in misery, and you let anybody who listens know it.

You feel depressed or anxious. Sometimes depression is clinical. Other times it's a symptom of struggling to live an inauthentic life. You are battling emotions that you can't explain. Feelings of sadness, darkness, and being overwhelmed, regardless of what you do to try to feel happy, are indications that something in your life needs to change.

NOT LIKING YOUR LIFE IS ENOUGH REASON TO CHANGE IT

I know I've shared some of my traumatic experiences and how the bad things that have happened in my life became my catalyst for change. Maybe you can relate to some of them. You may have survived abuse and abandonment too. And maybe you haven't. Either way, it's okay.

You don't need a traumatic experience to change your life. But you do need the desire to change.

Maybe you want to throw your entire life in the trash and create a new one. Maybe there is one area that you really need to change, like your health or your career.

Your "what" doesn't matter. If it's uncomfortable for you, then it has to go. If it doesn't feel good to you anymore, that is all that matters.

This is *your* life.

YOU'RE STUCK, AND IT SHOWS

Our lives are a direct reflection of the decisions and subsequent moves we don't make. Sometimes we stay stuck due to our mindset, and sometimes it's that we can't get our behavior to line up with what we want. More often than not, it's a combination of the two.

We've talked a lot about why your life isn't where you want it to be. If it hasn't started to click as to why you're still stuck in a place you hate and can't seem to move, here are the primary reasons why you've stayed stuck this long:

- **Your life is fucked up, but it's comfortable**. Here's that truth again. You're scared to take a step toward a new life.
- **You haven't done counseling or therapy**. You're trying to build a house with no tools. You're out here swimming in the deep end of the pool with no floaties. You've been trying to

change your life without the proper and professional support you need.

- **You are passing the blame.** It's still everybody else's fault but yours. You're looking outward instead of inward for the reasons why your life is not where you want it to be when the truth is if you don't like your life, if you're feeling bad about where you are, then it's nobody else's fault but yours. The only question is: What do you need to do to change it? Radical responsibility, remember?
- **You haven't met the right person to call you out on your shit.** It's so much easier and safer to surround yourself with people who let you get away with being mediocre. People who pucker up and kiss your ass. People who play small and allow you to do the same. And you keep those people around because...
- **You're scared of hurting people who you know can't come with you.** Even though you know most of your current circle isn't conducive to your growth, you don't want to hurt them by cutting them off. It's easier to let the possibility of their hurt feelings hold you back.

If you haven't started to address these areas, go back to the earlier chapters of this book and do that work.

But once you've decided that you're willing to be uncomfortable, started the therapy you need, and cleaned house in your personal life, you can move on to the last reason why you are stuck:

- **You're not clear on what you want (and don't).** You can't get to a goal that you haven't defined.

Let's get to that.

WHAT DO YOU WANT?

Now you're ready to get really clear on what you want. Before we start defining what you want your life to look and feel like, I want to give you a few important tips:

Don't skip too far ahead. What you want today may not be what you want tomorrow or 10 years from now. What do you want right now, at this moment? Focus on that versus the far future.

Release the idea of comfort. I can't stress this enough. If you limit your vision for yourself and your life to what you think is attainable, you are putting yourself out of the game before you even start. Accept the fact that shift may feel like shit. No pain, no gain.

Be super specific. Vague is not good here. Your goals can't be gray. You need to be honest and clear about what you want, including what you'll never want to go back to again.

My entire life changed when I got really clear on the life I wanted to live and laid it out so I could feel it and see it.

This is what that looks like:

- I want a business that allows me to impact people.
- I want to be successful on my own terms.
- I want to be sure my family is happy, healthy, very well taken care of, and we're not living paycheck-to-paycheck.
- I want us to have a better life than I had.

And as clear as I am about what I want, I am equally as clear on what I don't want:

- I don't want to live with that feeling of despair that I always had growing up.
- I don't want to be worried about how we were going to get to the next dollar.

So I will do what I need to do to make sure I never have to live that kind of life again.

Now it's your turn. Let's start with one of my favorite, most powerful techniques I learned from Tony Robbins for creating lasting change in your life. This shit isn't for the faint of heart, but if you're ready to do the work, it can be a game-changer.

Close your eyes and imagine your life five, 10, 20 years from now if you don't make a change. Really feel that pain, that despair, that sense of being trapped in a life you hate. Don't sugarcoat it. Let it get raw and real.

Now, flip the script. Imagine a different future, one where you've made the changes you need to make. You're living the life you've always dreamed of, feeling fulfilled, proud, and at peace. Let yourself get lost in that feeling of joy, excitement, and accomplishment.

Here's the thing: Your brain is powerful. It can't tell the difference between what's real and what's vividly imagined. So when you do this exercise, you're actually training your mind to link massive pain to staying stuck and massive pleasure to making a change.

That's some powerful shit right there. When you associate enough pain with something, you'll move heaven and earth to avoid it. And when you associate enough pleasure with something, you'll do whatever it takes to get it.

But let's be real. You can't just do this exercise once and expect your life to magically transform. You've got to make it a nonnegotiable part of your daily routine. Take a few minutes every day to close your eyes and really feel the pain of staying stuck and the pleasure of changing.

Over time, something dope starts to happen. Your brain starts to rewire itself, breaking free from those old patterns of self-sabotage and procrastination. Taking action toward your goals starts to feel like second nature.

So don't sleep on this simple but powerful exercise. It could be the key to unlocking the change you've been hungry for.

But let's keep it 100 percent real. Change is never easy. It's uncomfortable, it's terrifying, it's uncertain as fuck. But it's also the only way to create the life you truly want. So you've got to be willing to get uncomfortable. You've got to be willing to face your fears head-on. You've got to be willing to put in the work, day after day because on the other side of that discomfort is everything you've ever wanted.

And you, my friend, are worth it. You deserve to live a life that lights you up from the inside out. So let's get to work.

CHAPTER TWO SELF-ASSESSMENT: LIFE WHEEL REALNESS

Think through what you want your life to look and feel like. Once you've done that, let's dive into this Life Wheel exercise. This is about taking a long, hard look at your life and figuring out what areas need some serious attention.

Grab a pen and paper, and let's break this down:

1. Draw a big-ass circle on your paper. This is your Life Wheel.
2. Divide that circle into eight slices, like you're cutting a pizza. Label each slice with an area of your life that matters to you. We're talking health, relationships, career, finances, personal growth, spirituality, fun and recreation, and physical environment. If there's an area that's important to you but not on this list, add it in.
3. Now, here's where the realness comes in. On a scale of 1-10, rate your current level of satisfaction in each area. One means "This area of my life is a total dumpster fire," and 10 means "I'm killing it and couldn't be happier." Be honest with yourself. If your health is a three, own that shit.
4. Once you've rated each area, color in each slice up to the level you rated it. Use a different color for each slice. When

you're done, take a step back and look at your wheel. Is it a smooth ride, or is that thing wobbling all over the place?
5. Here's the part that might sting a little: Write down why you rated each area the way you did. What's working? What's not? What do you need to change? Don't hold back. This is your life we're talking about.
6. Now, imagine your ideal life. What would a 10 look like in each area? Write that down too. Get specific. What would you be doing? How would you be feeling? Who would you be surrounded by?
7. Look at the gap between your current ratings and your ideal life. That's where you need to focus your energy. Pick one or two areas to start with. What's one small action you can take today to move closer to your ideal in that area? Write it down, and then go do it.

Listen up, this exercise isn't a one-and-done deal. Your Life Wheel is a living, breathing thing. Revisit it regularly. Check in with yourself. Celebrate your progress. Adjust your course when needed.

And remember, creating a life that feels good all around takes time and effort. You're not going to go from a three to a 10 in your health overnight. But every small action you take is a step in the right direction.

This is your life, and you only get one shot at it. You deserve to live a life that feels good, that lights you up, that makes you excited to jump out of bed in the morning.

So take a good, hard look at your Life Wheel. Get real about where you are and where you want to be. And then start taking action, one small step at a time.

You've got this. Now let's get to work on creating a life that's a smooth ride all around.

3

RADICAL HONESTY

Redefining yourself and your life requires something that few of us have had the heart to do, and that is to get honest. Really honest. *Radically* honest. About everyone and everything. Starting with the person that you simultaneously know the best and the least—yourself.

Radical honesty is getting to the bottom of it all, having that long overdue, heart-to-heart talk you know you need to have with yourself but you've been ducking and dodging for way too long.

It's the process where you pick it all apart, take a good hard look at where you are, how you got here, and most importantly, how in the hell you get out of a life that you want to leave behind.

WHO ARE YOU REALLY?

A lot happened in your life between birth and age 7. The most critical time in a child's life, this is the phase of your development that had the most impact on who you became.

From the time you were born, you were being shaped and molded into who someone else wanted you to be.

Think about it. At a young age, someone else—your parents, grandparents, or teachers—made most of your decisions for you.

You were told what to do. You were told what to wear. You were told what to eat and when. You were told what to do and what time to do it.

Those decisions and that direction became your thoughts and beliefs. Your compass and your conditioning. Everything important about you and to you was dictated by the adults around you. And that means *everything*.

Your value systems and your beliefs. Your God. Your dreams of who you wanted to be when you grew up and who you decided to be. Everything that you've determined to be important in life was already established by everyone else around you.

When it comes to your identity, who and what you are, it's been imposed on you or you've inherited it. Either way, you did not choose it.

Part of the work of redefining yourself is to get to the truth of who you really are by taking a deep look into why you think what you think and do what you do, and also by removing the limitations that have been placed on you and that you've placed on yourself as a result. You have to evaluate everything, even the personality that you've adopted. What you've told yourself is your personality is a pattern of practicing protection.

You are protecting yourself from discomfort, more trauma, hurt, disappointment, or fear.

You call yourself an introvert so you don't have to be in social situations that scare and stretch you.

You say you're not smart so when you fail that class because you didn't work hard, not because you couldn't, you or no one else is surprised.

You say you're bad at math so you don't have to take responsibility for your money.

Is this who you are, really? If you didn't have to protect yourself anymore, who would you be? Pick your personality apart and get real.

CHAPTER THREE SELF-ASSESSMENT: THE REAL YOU

Answer these questions:

1. Is how I am showing up in my life who I really am?
2. What are the parts of my personality that feel forced?
3. In what ways am I trying to fit an image (positive or negative) that isn't me?
4. Who do I want to be?
5. How do I want to see myself?
6. Am I living the life that I want, or am I stuck in something that someone else wanted for me?

If your answers above revealed that there is a disconnect between who you are and who you want to be, good. That's exactly why you're here. You are here to become less defined by who you believe you should be and more defined by who you want to be.

For too long, your choices about your life and what you want to do with it haven't been yours. To redefine yourself, you have to change that.

WHOSE LIFE ARE YOU LIVING ANYWAY?

I have a big question for you. It's a question that you've probably never asked yourself or thought about before.

It's a question that will force you to examine everything about your life up until this point.

A question that forces you to pick your life up by the legs, flip it upside down, and shake it until everything falls out of the pockets.

Here it is: Why do you want what you want?

I bet you've never really thought about where and how you live your life and how many of those decisions are not actually yours.

Have you borrowed somebody else's vision for your life?

The life that you're living, are you living it because you actually want it or because someone else wanted it for you?

Is it because you saw the life that the people you look up to lived— your family, your teachers—so you decided that you needed a life that looked like theirs?

Is it because they had a dream for you and decided that you would live it? Your parents never went to college, so they want you to. But what if you want to go to culinary school to become a chef?

Your parents worked their jobs for 30 years and have been able to make a decent living so as far as they are concerned, college is a waste of money. But what if you want to escape your small town to go away to college, live on a campus, and have the time of your life? What if college is the path to your dream of working on Wall Street?

Are you going to forgo your future for your family members who can't see anything beyond their front porch? Are you going to allow traditions to tell you what to do?

Is your life a reflection of the roles that have been defined for you?

Are you who you are and where you are because of what our society expects? Society says because you are a woman, you have to be married and a mother.

Or what about if you are poor, your life is never supposed to amount to anything. Or if you are rich, do you have to live in a certain type of house or drive a certain car? Or if you graduate from high school, you have to go to college?

Are you going to allow old stories and society's "rules" that say people of a certain income who live in a certain neighborhood or are a certain color and look a certain way have to have a certain life to decide who you are and who you get to be? Are you going to live by their rules or your own?

This is your life, and you get to choose everything in it. Nothing that you've been until this point defines who you are if you don't want it to—including your DNA.

While I was in the process of writing this book, I found out that the man who I thought was my biological father wasn't.

I actually found out by accident. If it were my mother's decision, I never would have known.

My family isn't unique in that it has its share of secrets. I knew some of them. For example, my grandmother on my father's side of the family was adopted, something that I found out later in life too. Looking back, maybe that should have given me a clue to dig deeper into my family line, but I didn't think much of it at the time.

Fast forward years later, I'd decided to take one of those ancestry tests to find out what parts of the world my family was from. My mother used to talk about how we had Native Americans in our family and of course, as a Black woman, I knew we had African ancestry as well. Exploring all of that was supposed to be a fun research project to draw out my family tree, not something that unraveled my identity and who I thought I'd come from and, in some ways, who I thought I was.

Although I never lived with the man who I thought was my father, he was such a significant part of my life. He was locked up in New York while I was stuck in California with my mother. But despite the distance, he was always there, you know? Like a lifeline, a promise that one day he'd get out and save me from the hell I was living in.

But then, plot twist. He died when I was 14, in December of that year. And just to add an extra kick in the teeth from the universe, I got yanked out of my home and tossed into foster care the very next month. Why? Because I finally found the courage to tell the police about the sexual abuse.

So there I was, 14 years old, and the two things I was holding onto—the hope that my dad would come rescue me, and the familiar chaos of my home life—both gone in a blink. I felt like I was in free fall, like the ground had been ripped out from under me.

Until he died, I always held on to the hope that my father would be released from prison and come to save me from the hell I was living in with my mother. Whenever I talked to him, he reminded me that he would take me from California back to New York, where he and my grandmother was from. We would be a family.

That never happened.

Now here I am, a 30-something-year-old woman, and my dreams of my father died for a second time as I read through my DNA results. All of these unfamiliar faces and names appeared. None of them were the father that I knew.

When I told my mother about what I'd found out, she barely acknowledged it, much less comforted me. That didn't surprise me. But what she said next did.

Instead of sharing what she knew about my real father and his relationship with me, she decided it was time to reveal another secret that she'd been keeping.

When she got pregnant with me at about 14 years old, she was also being molested at home. What she shared shocked me into silence for so many reasons. To find out that we'd been sexually abused at the same age unnerved me in ways that I couldn't explain. To think that traumatic history had been passed down from one generation to the next was surreal to me. Being sexually abused was not an experience that I ever thought I'd have in common with my own mother.

I spent the next 48 hours processing everything that I'd learned about myself.

This was my family, my blood, the people who'd made me, or at least that's what I'd always thought.

If I'm being honest, I always felt different. But never in a million years did I think that was because I didn't belong to my father by blood. It wasn't my fault, but I had been living a lie for my entire life.

I had to decide how this was going to affect me now that I knew the truth. This new information forced me to sit with myself, with who I thought I was, and reconcile that with who I *knew* I was.

Don't ask me to recite a Bible verse, but I am a very spiritual person. I could feel God and my guardian angel, my grandmother, right there, assuring me that what I'd found out about my family didn't matter.

In my body and my heart, I kept hearing God and my grandmother speaking to me. I heard the words I needed to hear: "None of this matters. I still love you."

In their eyes, I hadn't changed. I had to see myself through those same eyes. I realized I was the same woman I was before I learned about my father. As hard as it was to find out, I was able to come back to myself. I did what I've always done. I decided who I was going to be—again.

It didn't matter whose DNA I had. It couldn't change the woman I was today, tomorrow, or 20 years from now. My life, as beautiful as it is, is far more of a reflection of my decisions than my DNA. My bloodline doesn't define me. Who I was born to be defines me, and there is nothing that could change that. Unless I let it.

My life, your life, is determined by who we decide to be. Nothing that anyone can do or say can change that.

LIVING UP TO LABELS

Until we know better, our identity is shaped not by who we think or know we are. It's shaped by who we've been told to be.

To redefine yourself, you have to get back to who you were supposed to be—the person that God intended for you to be.

Who you were born to be is your baseline. You are here to be who you were created to be, not what you've been called.

We all have a "they" in our lives. They are the people who were determined to put all of you in a box, even if it was intended to protect you, without allowing you to discover who you were meant to be. The people who doubted you. The people who discouraged and derailed you. The people who discounted you. The people who disappointed you.

All of these people have called you something other than what you are. You have to discover who you were before they told you who you should be. Who were you before they put their label on you?

You can take the label off. You can decide who you are. What you have been called all of your life – not smart, not disciplined, not destined to be rich or successful—whatever it was, is irrelevant.

Remove that label from yourself and live the life you want to and the life you were created to live.

"IT'S NOT WHAT THEY CALL YOU, IT'S WHAT YOU ANSWER TO"

From an early age, I was labeled a liar.

It started with my mother. She has devalued me all of my life. In her mind, she decided who I was and who I was going to be—nothing. To her, I was insubordinate and insignificant. She never believed anything I said.

When her boyfriend, who abused me, walked me right into her room and dared me to tell her what he was doing to me, there wasn't a doubt in her mind that I was lying when I told her the truth. To this day, my mother refers to what happened as "an affair." She has convinced herself that, as a 14-year-old girl, I had an affair with her 20-something-year-old boyfriend.

Not having my own mother believe me was almost as traumatic as the abuse itself. She didn't cover and protect me. She didn't take my side. She didn't yell and fight this man, call the police, or even put him out of our house. Instead, he got to stay, and I was taken away.

I knew I didn't deserve to be molested. I knew the man was wrong for what he did to me.

But somehow, when she called me a liar, I took that on. Deep down, I believed it. And for years, I believed that everyone else would believe it too. There was no use in trying to convince the world that I was different.

My mother wasn't the only one who labeled me a liar in my life.

When you are a little Black girl from the hood, people make a lot of assumptions about who you are. Girls are already sexualized at a very early age, and that happens even earlier for girls who live in ghettos like I did.

Society assumes that based on how you look, how quickly your butt and boobs develop, or based on where you live that you are open to anything and anyone sexually.

In my freshman year of school, my home life was chaotic. I was in foster care. Being away from my brothers and sisters—even my mother, as unstable as she was—was much harder than I thought it would be. I was so worried about the other kids. As the oldest, I'd always felt responsible for them. For as long as I can remember, I was the matriarch of our family. When my mother would fall apart, at least they had me to hold it—and us—together. I protected them as best I could, but then there was nothing that I could do.

My foster mother hadn't put her hands on me, but she wasn't interested in being the nurturing mother that I needed. She made it clear from day one that I was pretty much on my own. I went from one unprotected place to another.

First day at my new foster home I was informed by my foster mother that I wouldn't be given a key to her house. She told me that whatever I did, I'd better not come back to her house before 5:30 p.m. because that was the time she would be home from work. So from the time I left the house until 5:30pm, I had nowhere to go. I had to find something to do with myself until I could go home, so I decided to run track.

After practice one afternoon, a guy approached me. I'd seen him around school and the field before, and I'd noticed him watching me. He was smiling, and so I smiled back. Flattered, I was thinking exactly like a 14-year-old would.

He likes me.

A boy liked *me*. That was all I knew and all I cared about at the moment. He was giving me attention, and I ate up every bit of it.

Naivete is like a scent. Men can smell the insecurity all over you. Despite all the mouth and attitude I had, I was really shy. At that point in my life, I didn't feel attractive enough to be around guys and knew nothing about how to handle myself around them.

My mom didn't play when it came to me and boys, or anybody else outside of family, to be honest, so I was really sheltered too. When this boy took me by the hand and asked me to come to sit in his car, I was so caught up in the attention that I didn't think that he wanted to do anything more than talk. Of course, he had other plans.

We'd been sitting in his car for a while when tried to make a move. He reached over and tried to slide his hand up my track shorts. I was immediately triggered. I froze. But unlike my mother's boyfriend, I wasn't going to take his shit. Nobody was going to take my body without my permission again. I didn't want him touching me, and I told him. I jumped out of the car and ran.

As I walked down the hall at school the next day, it was like I was in a rom-com scene. I could feel all of these eyes on me and hear people whispering. Finally, I found out what was up.

The asshole told everyone that I'd had sex with him in his car.

When I tried to tell people what really happened, nobody would believe me. So I stopped trying to tell the truth.

I allowed them to tell lies about me. I didn't tell a lie. But I lived one. I let the lie exist without bothering to try to campaign to convince anyone to change their mind.

If people were going to call me a liar, then I would be one. I didn't bother correcting people, and I let the label live on me.

Liar. Hoe. Stupid ghetto girl. Loud. Poor. Worthless. Insignificant. All of those are labels that people put on me, and I allowed it.

The problem with labels is they become lies.

If we're not careful, we subconsciously start to become the person we've been labeled as. That is how lies become limitations.

And limitations keep us little.

Little sense of self-worth and self-perception.

Little dreams.

Little education.

Little money.

Little lives when we know we're meant for so much more.

I am not a liar. In fact, I am one of the most honest people you'll ever meet. Have I lied in my life? Yes. But I am not a liar.

I am also not a sexually promiscuous, poor, ghetto girl who would never do anything with her life but have a bunch of babies and live on welfare.

I am nothing like the little girl that my family, and even some of my childhood friends, labeled me.

My friends know me as Lakeysha Cobbs. But I have a whole new identity, life, and even an additional last name.

LaKeysha Cobbs is still a part of my life, but who they think I am doesn't represent me anymore. I left that little girl a long time ago. She is a past life, a past version of me.

I learned what I needed to learn from that life, from that little girl, and I've moved on.

I don't have to be who they think I am or who anyone else does, either.

I am me—the me that I've decided to be. I get to reinvent and redefine myself whenever and however I choose to.

You can take the labels off. Think about the jar of spaghetti sauce that is in your pantry right now. We can take the label off of that jar and pour it into a bowl. We can add more ingredients to the same sauce. Now it's something new, something better, something more than before.

You get to be whoever and whatever you want to be. The person that you started out as when a child or even who you were yesterday is not who you have to be. Take what you needed to learn from that life and that version of yourself and build on it. Learn from it and become something else.

KEEPING IT REAL WHEN SHIT GETS REAL

Let's be real. This whole redefining yourself thing sounds great on paper, but when you actually start doing the work, it can get messy as hell. You're going to come up against some resistance, both from the people around you and from your own damn mind.

Your family and friends might not be too thrilled when you start questioning everything and making changes. They're used to you being a certain way, and your growth might make them uncomfortable. They might try to pull you back into old patterns and labels. That's when you've got to be radically honest with them and with yourself. You've got to stand firm in your truth and keep pushing forward, even when they're pushing back.

And then there's the resistance that comes from inside. Your mind is going to throw up all kinds of doubts and fears when you start stepping into unfamiliar territory. You might find yourself thinking, "Who the hell do I think I am, trying to be someone new? What if I fail? What if everyone laughs at me?" That's when you've got to call bullshit on those thoughts. You've got to be radically honest about the fact that those fears are just stories your mind is telling you, not reality.

But here's the thing: You don't have to do this alone. Surround yourself with people who have your back, who believe in your vision for yourself, and who will call you out when you're falling back into old patterns. Find a community of people who are on the same path of growth and self-discovery. Lean on them when shit gets tough, and celebrate with them when you break through to new levels.

Speaking of breaking through, let's talk about what's possible when you commit to radical honesty and redefining yourself. I'm not just talking about little changes here and there. I'm talking about complete fucking transformation. I'm talking about waking up one day and hardly recognizing the person you used to be because you've grown so much. I'm talking about creating a life that looks nothing like the one you were living before because you had the courage to question everything and create something new.

That's the power of radical honesty. When you're willing to get real with yourself about who you are, who you've been, and who you want to be, you open up a world of possibilities. You start living life on your own terms, not anyone else's. You start creating your own reality, instead of just reacting to circumstances.

So yeah, it might get messy. You might lose some people along the way. You might face some challenges and setbacks. But when you stay committed to your truth, when you keep peeling back the layers and redefining yourself, you'll find a freedom and a power you never knew you had. And that, my friend, is worth all the discomfort and all the work. Trust me.

Alright, let's dive into an exercise that's going to help you get radically honest with yourself about what really matters to you. This is about figuring out your nonnegotiables, the things that make you tick, the values that drive you. When you know what those are, you can start making decisions and setting goals that are in line with your authentic self.

CHAPTER THREE SELF-ASSESSMENT: GETTING REAL ABOUT WHAT MATTERS MOST

Grab your journal or a piece of paper, and let's do this.

1. Write down a list of your core values. These are the principles that guide your life, the things that are most important to you. We're talking about things like freedom, growth, connection, creativity, honesty, adventure, service, and so on. Don't censor yourself, just let the values flow.
2. Now look at your list and circle the top five values that resonate with you the most. These are the ones that feel like a "Hell yes!" in your gut.
3. For each of your top five values, write down what it means to you. What does it look like to embody this value in your life? For example, if one of your values is freedom, what does freedom mean to you? Is it financial freedom? The freedom to travel? The freedom to express yourself authentically?
4. Now here's where radical honesty comes in. Look at your life as it is right now—your relationships, your career, your daily habits, your choices. Are they aligned with your core values? Are you living in a way that honors what matters most to you?
5. If there are areas of your life that feel out of alignment with your values, write them down. Get specific. For example, if one of your values is growth but you've been stuck in the same dead-end job for years, write that down.
6. For each area that feels out of alignment, ask yourself: What would it look like to make a change that honors my values? What's one small step I could take to start bringing my life into greater alignment?
7. Make a commitment to yourself to start taking those steps, one day at a time. Use your values as your compass, guiding you toward the life you truly want to create.

This exercise isn't a one-and-done kind of thing. Your values might shift and evolve over time, and that's okay. The point is to keep checking in with yourself, keep being radically honest about what matters most to you, and keep making choices that are in alignment with your authentic self.

Here's the thing: When you're living in alignment with your values, you feel fucking amazing. You feel like you're in flow, like you're doing what you're meant to be doing. And that's what this whole redefining yourself thing is all about—creating a life that feels good, that feels true, that feels like YOU.

So get real about what matters most to you. Use that clarity to guide your actions and your choices. And watch as your life starts to transform in ways you never even imagined.

Remember, this list is not exhaustive. You may have values that are not included here. The purpose of this exercise is to help you identify the values that resonate most deeply with you and to use them as a guide for living a life that feels authentic and meaningful.

Take your time with this exercise. Reflect on each value and consider how it shows up (or doesn't show up) in your life currently. Think about how you can cultivate and express these values more fully in your daily thoughts, actions, and interactions.

Use your values as a filter for making decisions—from the big, life-changing ones to the small, everyday choices. When faced with a decision, ask yourself: Which choice aligns most closely with my values?

Remember that living your values is a lifelong practice. It requires ongoing self-reflection, honesty, and commitment. But when you align your life with your values, you create a powerful sense of purpose, fulfillment, and inner peace.

So get clarity on your values, and let them guide you toward a life that feels truly and unapologetically like **YOU**.

BONUS CONTENT: VALUES LIST

LIST 1	LIST 2	LIST 3	LIST 4
Authenticity	Abundance	Collaboration	Creativity
Balance	Adventure	Compassion	Curiosity
Commitment	Ambition	Connection	Empowerment
Consistency	Assertiveness	Contribution	Enlightenment
Courage	Autonomy	Empathy	Entrepreneurship
Determination	Boldness	Equality	Excellence
Discipline	Bravery	Fairness	Exploration
Efficiency	Challenge	Family	Flexibility
Focus	Clarity	Forgiveness	Freedom
Growth	Confidence	Friendship	Fulfillment
Honesty	Decisiveness	Generosity	Happiness
Humility	Determination	Gratitude	Harmony
Integrity	Enthusiasm	Growth	Imagination
Loyalty	Excitement	Helpfulness	Independence
Optimism	Fearlessness	Honesty	Individuality
Perseverance	Flexibility	Hope	Ingenuity
Reliability	Freedom	Humility	Innovation
Resilience	Independence	Inclusivity	Inspiration
Responsibility	Inspiration	Joy	Intuition
Self-Discipline	Motivation	Kindness	Leadership

4

RESISTANCE TO REDEFINING

RESISTANCE TRAINING IS ONE OF THE MOST EFFECTIVE WAYS TO BUILD muscle and physically redefine your body. Weights, special bands, and sometimes your own body weight is used to force your muscles to push against a strong force that, over time, will strengthen those muscles.

If you've done resistance training before, you know how hard it is, especially in the beginning. Regardless of the equipment that you're using, it seems easy at first, especially if you're working with the right personal trainer who you've hired to take you from couch potato to centerfold.

As trained professionals, they know that muscle-building is a process that takes time. If someone experiences too much pain too soon, it reduces the chances of them hanging in there long enough to start to see real results because who in their right mind shows up somewhere to do something knowing they'll have to hurt?

But slowly, over time, you'll feel yourself becoming stronger. What once felt like a struggle for you or arguably impossible will become easier. Be it bands or machines, the weights aren't lighter, you're stronger. Incrementally you've increased the amount of resistance that you're able to handle, and it shows. Your newer, stronger body is developing and bringing your mind along for the ride.

You kept pushing, and it paid off. You somehow found the will to persist when everything in you wanted to resist. Instead of running from the resistance, you ran to it and, eventually, through it. This is what the redefined version of you is made of.

Now, all we need to do is get you there.

RESISTANCE CAN MAKE OR BREAK YOU

By definition, the word "resistance" means "a refusal to accept or to comply with something."

Deciding that you want your life to look different in some way is a good first step. You want to change something. You get up every day feeling trapped, suffocated in a life, a career, a body, a relationship (maybe all of these) that you want to change. You feel it. You see it.

But being open to the idea of changing doesn't mean that you are open to doing what it takes to make that change a reality in your life. Wanting something is one thing. Being willing to change it is something else.

So, you have a decision to make:

Door #1: You can refuse to accept the life you have (that you hate) and get with the program to make something different happen.

Door #2: You can refuse to accept and comply with the change that is required to trash that life and live a different one.

Both options are a form of resistance. Will you choose the resistance that makes you into the person that you want to be (you guessed it, that's Door #1) or the resistance that breaks you and keeps you trapped right where you are? Resistance can make you strong or make you stuck—and you get to choose.

Make no mistake: You have a lot to break to get to your breakthrough. There's your past trauma. There are family and friend patterns and their pressure to do what, as a collective, you've always done. There's your fear about what you don't know and the new knowledge that you may need to succeed in the new spaces you're going to. There's the worry about potentially losing or leaving behind the person (or, in most cases, the people) who won't have a page in the next chapter of your life and if you'll ever find new friends or a partner.

And there's your comfort.

It may be hard to accept and to hear, but many of us believe that we are far more open to change than we really are. As much as you hate the misery and mediocrity that you're living in, you will probably hate the discomfort that it will take to change it more. It takes way more courage and effort to get out of comfort than it does to stay in it.

While we know there is more and better for us out there in this big world, the small, comfortable corner that we currently exist in has its benefits. It's warm and cozy. It's a lot less scary. It's predictable and familiar. It's controllable.

Regardless of how much you don't like your life, it's still the one that you know.

In the life that you have, you've learned it inside out. You know how to navigate all the landmines.

You know how to skate by on just enough so you can hold on to what you have.

You know how much risk you can take—or not—so you don't get hurt or lose too much.

You know to play it safe.

Even the most chaotic lives, the lives that we are struggling to survive in, are still easier to live because we know exactly what to do to keep them.

The Truth: Familiar chaos can be more comfortable than unfamiliar change.

Or in the BS advice (sorry mothers, it's true) from millions of mommas around the world, "The devil you know is better than the devil you don't."

Whatever your current chaos or devil is, it is far less frightening than the hell your mind has convinced you is necessary to change—even when your life is on the line.

Let's imagine a rock climber is out for a climb on a sunny morning. She's been climbing almost all her life, so she feels she can do this with her eyes closed. She starts climbing. One arm, one foot at a time, she hoists her well-conditioned body up, bit by bit. She's moving as she normally does, confident and assured.

I've got this, she thinks to herself as she smiles between grunts.

And then the unimaginable happens. Despite having conquered mountains like this a few times before on her own, she starts slipping. In what feels like an instant, she finds herself hanging off the cliff. Feet dangling 30 feet in the air, she's paralyzed with fear.

Gripping the edge with both hands, her bleeding nails are digging deep into the rock, fighting to hold on with everything she has. Too afraid to look down, her eyes are clenched tight.

Out of nowhere, the climber looks up to see an angel, a stranger, standing above her.

"Take it!" the person yells while dangling a rope. "Grab it with your hand!"

The climber can't move, even though she knows her weakening arms won't be able to hold her much longer. She slowly pulls one of her hands away from the cliff's edge, testing her strength. As soon as she does, fear convinces her that there is no way she can hold on long enough to grab the rope just above her head.

Even with the assurance of her biceps that have never failed her before, she fears the unlikely possibility of falling to her death more

RESISTANCE TO REDEFINING

than she trusts her body, the rope, and the stranger lifting her to safety. She hangs there, screaming, and crying until she can't hold on anymore.

I'll let you guess how that story ends.

Many of us would read a story like that, shaking our heads in disbelief. We would judge this woman, calling her all kinds of stupid, swearing that there was no way that we would make a grave mistake like that, choosing an inevitable fall to our death out of fear.

But before you join that club, I want you to think about something. How many ropes have you refused to grab in your own life out of fear?

Your work bestie leaves the job and the asshole manager you both spent countless lunch hours venting to each about, but you won't send her your resume when she begs you to apply for the position— the one that would be perfect for you—at her new company.

That's a rope.

Your college school sweetheart and the undeniable love of your life stays in your inbox, professing their love for you, but you won't give them the time of day because you're praying that the no-good-narcissistic-serial-cheater that you've been with for seven years will finally realize how valuable you are.

That's a rope.

Won't fill out the application for the scholarship you would be a shoo-in for? *Rope.*

Fear of the unknown will make us believe that holding on to what little we have is a better bet than fighting our fears, grabbing the rope that's being thrown at us, and going after what could be possible— even when our lives are dependent on it.

We would rather hang to the edge of our lives as we know them, clinging to certainty and comfort in a death grip as we watch our lives flash before our eyes than let go, grab that rope, and trust in it—and ourselves—to pull us up and out of the mess that our fear has us living in.

Or, in the words of lecturer and author Dr. Joe Dispenza, "We would rather cling to our suffering than take a risk on possibility."

Suffering doesn't always mean pain, at least not in the literal sense of the word. Suffering looks different for all of us.

Whether it's sitting in a cubicle that you know is too small to hold your life's purpose, harming your body with unhealthy habits like overeating or drinking too much when you know you need to change, or not leaving an abusive relationship, suffering shows up in our lives in different ways. No matter how you slice it or what it looks like, for you, suffering is suffering.

So why do we stay in it?

The Truth: If you stay suffering long enough, it eventually feels like safety.

When it comes to making decisions, many of which you make on autopilot, keeping yourself safe drives a lot of your day-to-day choices.

Your natural response is to stick with what's safest and most predictable in life, even if it is completely chaotic. To keep yourself out of harm's way. To not rock the boat so much that you fall into the ocean and drown.

It may look easy for some people, but taking risks is not something that comes naturally. Taking a chance is a learned behavior. When given an opportunity to do something new, if risk is not your thing, you'll want to talk yourself out of it. The warning bells in your mind start screaming, "Wait! What if I go over there and...

I'm too stupid to do this?"

I'm not good at this?"

I get laughed at?"

It doesn't work, and I fail?"

They get mad at me for leaving, and now I'm alone?"

I can't find someone new who likes or loves me?"

What you thought were legitimate reasons why you should not do that thing you know would move you one step closer to a goal and the life you want was really your body and mind's response to the fear it perceives when you want to do anything outside of your comfort zone.

When you are detouring from your norm, your mind will do its job and raise a red flag. Your job is to distinguish between what's different for you and what's dangerous and unsafe for you and act accordingly.

Safety does not want you to win if it means coloring outside the lines and living outside of the confines of your comfort zone. Your safety senses are fine when you're in true danger. But when we're talking about redefining yourself, safety is standard. Safety is simply survival. Safety is stuck.

What keeps you safe is not what will help you be successful.

When the hair on the back of your neck stands up as you walk down a strange street in the dark toward a stranger holding a gun or tease a hungry lion in the jungle, trust that.

But when your fear is screaming at you to run away from the path pointing you to a different life, you should question that. In fact, you should run toward that very thing because it's likely to be a small—or huge—step that could change your life.

FEAR HAS A SOUND

We typically identify fear as a feeling—the butterflies in our bellies, sweat-stained underarms, or our hearts racing.

But fear also has a sound. It sounds like self-doubt and the stories you tell yourself about the things you can't do or have. It sounds like the criticism that you've heard so much that it became your own voice. It sounds like limitation.

You want to lose weight, but fear says, "Will my partner still love me if I look different?"

You want to make more money, but fear says, "If I make more money, I'll have to pay more taxes. I've always heard more money, more problems!"

You want to start that business, but that damn fear says, "I'll have to come from behind the scenes and be out front if I want to market my business. I hate how I look, and I know people will say mean things about me, so I need to hide."

Instead of focusing on what could work out for us, our minds will go to the most far-fetched outcome and the most unlikely scenario, aka the lies, that could happen.

It doesn't matter that we have absolutely no evidence or experience to prove that those outcomes are possible. The fear speaks so loud that it's impossible for us to hear anything else.

So we stay overweight, in careers and in spaces and situations that trap us, and unhappy instead of working toward the change that we want. We stay questioning if we have what it takes, if we are good enough, and if we can handle the pain that comes with change.

I want you to finish this book, but if I had to sum up everything that I need to tell you right now and give you the cheat code to changing your life, here it is:

The answer is yes. You do have what it takes, you are enough, and you can handle whatever it takes to redefine yourself.

Once you recognize the sound of your own fear, you'll know how to shut it up and shut it down when it comes. You'll know how to determine when your fear is feeding you lies and if that voice in your head that's screaming, "STOOOOOOP!" is just noise in response to the possibility of doing and becoming something new.

I know that the sound of fear has been so loud in your head for so long that it has drowned out anything that sounds like progress, possibility, or potential.

That shit stops today.

Turn it off.
When fear starts to come for you, remember:

It's a lie. Whatever fear is whispering in your ear to convince you not to pursue what you want, know that it's a lie. There are a million reasons why we know this to be true, starting with the fact that there are too many examples of success out there.

If it's possible for someone else, why wouldn't it be possible for you? There is nothing that you want that somebody in this world doesn't already have. If they can do it, why can't you?

It's not that you're not smart. You just haven't been taught the right way.

It's not that you can't lose weight. You just haven't found the right trainer or diet plan.

It doesn't matter how many times you or someone else has tried to convince you that you can't change. It's a lie. Know a lie when you hear one.

You haven't given yourself a real shot at winning. Before you count yourself out and claim that change is too hard, be honest with yourself. Have you really tried? Have you locked in on something and given it everything you had—and then some? Don't count yourself out before you even start. You've done that too many times before. We're moving differently now.

Focus on what you have done. I seriously doubt that you've never achieved anything good in your life. I don't care if it was an award for best art that you won in kindergarten. You've done something. In fact, you've done a lot of things. You have a track record. Fight fear with facts.

Refuse to back down. Never forget that your fear has one mission: To convince you to quit. It wants you to stop. To go back to where you came from and who you used to be. To hide. Fear is expecting you to give up and back down—again. But if you can square up and stare your fear in the face, even if you are shaking when you do it, and refuse to run away from it, you'll find that fear quiets down. Now fear is backing down, not you.

THE COST OF CLINGING TO COMFORTABLE

It's easy not to value something when we don't realize what it really costs. You may be making the mistake of discounting the cost of your freedom and living a life that's truly yours.

I want you to take a second and think about something. This may hurt a little but stay with me, alright?

I want you to think about everything that clinging to your comfort has cost you. And I mean *everything*. The years. The success. The love. The health. The happiness. The home. The family. The fun. The money. The memories.

If you had to put a price on all you've lost due to fear, what do you estimate your total to be?

I know. That number is way too big. It's likely beyond your comprehension and calculation. In fact, it may be priceless. But whatever that loss looks like for you, you know it's up there.

The bottom line is this: By constantly convincing yourself to choose certainty and comfort, you've lost too much. If you stay stuck where you are right now, there is still so much more for you to lose.

Are you willing to forgo your future? Are you willing to never know what it feels like to be free, to live the life that you've always wanted to live, the life you were born to live, because you refuse to let go? Are you willing to keep clinging to what's comfortable and what you've convinced yourself that you are capable of?

I know you're not.

The beauty of redefining yourself is that you now have a chance to get it all back. Redefining yourself is reclaiming your life.

Loosen up your grip on this comfortable life that you've settled for so you can step into the amazing life you deserve. Confront your comfort once and for all. Face your fear. Be willing to get uncomfortable.

RESISTANCE TO REDEFINING

Do different so you can become different.

When you're standing at the door of different—a different job, relationship, mindset, it doesn't matter what it is—you won't always know exactly what to say or do next, but you can know this for sure: Don't ever go back to where or who you were.

If you can fight the urge to resist being uncomfortable, to avoid what is new, your life will change. In the words of badass businesswoman and corporate executive Bozoma St. John: "It's uncomfortable because you've never been here before."

So what does that tell you? Eventually, what is uncomfortable and unknown will become natural to you.

The very thing that you are scared to do today—that thing that is testing your willingness to try to move, to set yourself free and live the life you really want to live, to fight for your right to redefine, to become the person that you really want to become—will be your testimony tomorrow.

Make no mistake, changing your life in a major way will likely be the hardest thing you'll ever do. Separating yourself from the pack you've always known to do something different from what you've always done is hard. Contradicting what you've always thought and who you've always been is hard. Feeling different, looking different, and talking and acting different is *hard*. It may take time. Tears. Trying and more trying— and even more trying.

You'll want to quit. You'll tell yourself you don't deserve it and you aren't worthy. You'll fuck shit up. (There's that self-sabotage again). You'll try to convince yourself that where you are now is better than where you could be. It's not. It's just easier. It's convenient. It's comfortable.

That comfort is why it's much easier to complain to friends, fill planners and journals with goals and dreams, watch Sunday sermons and do all the fasts and prayers, or suffer in silence than to commit to change.

If the idea of changing your life feels too hard for you, think about this:

You already know how this path plays out. Remember that list of what your comfort has cost you? That is a visual enough of what is at stake if you don't change. You know what your life will look like if you do nothing. What you don't know is what it will look like if you do *everything* you can to become a different version of yourself. Finding out is worth the risk, don't you think?

You've done hard shit before, and you can do more. Your life has taught you a lot, and one of those lessons is that you can and will make it. There are people who know your story and are scratching their heads, wondering how you're still here. If you can survive that, you can do anything. You've lived through some things and each time, you came out on the other side. You can and will do it again. You are made of much more than you think.

You want this. You're here because you know that your current life is not your best life. Yes, you've been making the best of the life you have. If you are reading this book, I know that *you* know that a better life is available to you. Don't punk out, please. Do what it takes to have it.

Alright, let's dive into a couple of powerful exercises that are going to help you punch resistance in the face and claim the life you deserve.

CHAPTER FOUR SELF-ASESSMENT: FLIP THE SCRIPT ON YOUR FEARS

We all have those bullshit beliefs that hold us back, those nagging voices that tell us we're not good enough, that we can't handle change, that we're destined to fail. Well, it's time to call those voices out and flip the script.

1. Grab your journal or a piece of paper and write down one limiting belief or fear that's been fueling your resistance to

change. Maybe it's something like, "I'm too old to start a new career" or "I'll never be able to lose this weight."
2. Now, I want you to look at that belief from a different angle. How could you see it differently? What's a more empowering way to look at your situation? For example:
   - "I have a wealth of experience and wisdom that will be valuable in any new career."
   - "I've overcome challenges before, and I can do it again. My age is an asset, not a limitation."
   - "Losing weight is a journey, and every small step I take is progress. I'm committed to my health, no matter how long it takes."
3. Write down your new, empowering belief and say it out loud. How does it feel? Repeat it to yourself daily, and watch how it starts to shift your perspective and your actions.

CHAPTER FOUR SELF-ASSESSMENT: TAP INTO YOUR INNER BADASS

We've all had moments in our lives when we felt like absolute badasses—when we pushed through fear, overcame a challenge, or achieved something we never thought possible. Those moments are powerful resources that we can tap into whenever we need a boost of courage or confidence.

1. Think back to a specific time when you felt like a total rockstar. Maybe it was when you nailed that presentation at work, when you stood up for yourself in a difficult conversation, or when you completed your first 5K race.
2. Close your eyes and fully immerse yourself in that memory. What did you see, hear, and feel? How did you carry

yourself? What was your inner dialogue like? Really relive that experience in vivid detail.
3. Now choose a physical representation—a simple gesture like pressing your thumb and forefinger together or touching your wrist. As you fully associate into that memory, engage your anchor and hold it for a few seconds.
4. Take a deep breath and open your eyes. Whenever you need a hit of that badass energy in the future, simply engage your anchor and let those empowering feelings flood your body and mind.

These exercises might seem simple, but don't underestimate their power. By consistently challenging your limiting beliefs and tapping into your inner resources, you'll start to rewire your brain for success and resilience.

So start flipping those scripts and anchoring in your "badassery." Your redefined life is waiting for you, and these tools will help you claim it with the confidence and courage you've had inside you all along.

5

RESILIENCE

ABUSE OF ANY KIND CHANGES YOU.
    I've been abused sexually, physically, and emotionally. I know that abuse is trauma that you learn to heal through, not from.

From the time I was 12 years old until I was 14, a man who lived in my house raped me. He groomed me at first, testing how far he could go.

It started with him sneaking into my room at night. I would wake up out of my sleep with his head between my legs, having oral sex with me. Eventually, that progressed to me giving him oral sex and then intercourse.

As any child would be, I was confused. I knew what he was doing to me was wrong, but didn't know what to do about it. He never told me not to tell my mother. He didn't have to. He knew I wouldn't. Like many abusers, he knew that I would never say anything to anyone and if I did, that no one—especially my mother—would believe me.

He knew that despite my hard exterior, my tough girl, I-don't-give-a-shit-about-nothing-or-nobody personality, I wanted and needed more than anything else to be really loved. He knew that deep inside, there was a little girl who felt unloved, unworthy, and unprotected. A little girl who was lost. A little girl who was always the one who fell through the cracks in that house. A little girl who was unseen.

My mother was abusive. Even though there would be breaks when someone lived with us, she would still explode. And he saw it. He saw how I would get the shit beat out of me for any reason that my mother decided justified it, from talking back to making too much noise to breathing. When she wasn't hitting us, she would punish us by forcing us to hold up stacks of encyclopedias for hours or filling our mouths with hot sauce.

It was almost two years before I told anyone that I was being sexually abused. When I started confiding in a girlfriend at school about it, she confirmed what I already knew: Everything about what was happening to me was wrong. Until she and I began talking about it, I wasn't willing to accept or admit it, mostly because I didn't really think I could do anything about it. Despite the fact that this man was old enough to be my father and was my mother's boyfriend, I felt trapped by the abuse. I shouldn't have been, but I was.

My friend started to make me see things differently. Talking to her gave me power. She pushed me to do something about what was happening. She told me to start locking my door and eventually convinced me to tell my mother. That was every bit of the disaster I thought it would be.

It actually happened after my abuser cornered me in the house. "Go tell her," he said, practically daring me to do it.

He walked me right into my mother's room and stood there, demanding that I tell her. I froze. She looked at me. I said nevermind and went back into my room. She wouldn't believe me. I was convinced she would do or say anything to keep this man, including sacrificing her own children—and herself.

Despite how abusive she could be, I always knew that my mother was fragile. So as a kid, I had one mission in life, and that was to protect her at all costs. I never wanted to upset her. I walked on eggshells, physically and emotionally, all the time. In my mind, that would prevent her from falling apart. Somehow I knew that if she was ever completely broken, she would never be able to piece herself back together again. Somehow I knew that I would be okay. She wouldn't or couldn't be.

If convincing herself that I was lying to her about her boyfriend and what he really was kept her whole, then so be it. She could choose to let a motherfucking monster in her bed.

But I didn't have to. I didn't have to allow this man to rape me whenever he felt like it. I could do something. I had no one else to stand up for me, so I had to stand up for myself.

I started locking my bedroom door at night. When I started refusing him and fighting back, he didn't just go away. My abuser tried everything, leaving money on my nightstand, constantly complimenting me, baiting me with whatever he knew I wasn't getting from my mother.

But I'd found my power, and I refused to give up to him again. My friend eventually helped me find the courage to go to the police. The strength that I didn't have, I gathered from her. The police held me at the station and questioned me about everything that was happening at home. I was told to go back home and expect that my mother's boyfriend would be arrested.

There was a part of me that hoped getting the police involved would end it all. My abuser would get locked up. My mother would be devastated to lose him and hate me, but I was used to that. The children they had together would miss their father. I could handle all of it, and it would be worth it to get him out of our house and my life.

When we all went home that night, my mother sat me down and told me that I would ruin his life for what I'd done. She wanted me to go back to the police and tell them that I'd lied. She still refused to accept that her boyfriend molested me. She was only focused on three things: Keeping him, keeping secrets, and keeping appearances. What happened in our house stayed in our house. We didn't tell our family business to anyone. Her man was an elder to me, and I should respect him no matter what.

I went back to the police station to try to undo it. I did what my mother told me to do and tried to recant my story. But it was too late. Child Protective Services was already involved. The level of detail that I'd given in my statements to the police about the abuse was too much for even the most imaginative, dishonest child to make up. They knew that.

My abuser was arrested, but later let go. And so was I... It was then that my mother told the courts that she didnt want me to come home. Within 24 hours, I was taken from my mother and placed into my grandmother's care then later a foster home because my grandfather said I was too much to handle and he didn't want any part of the situation.

My abuser stole so much from me then. My innocence and my identity. My ability to trust. My home. My sense of safety. My right to decide who I gave my body to, how, and when. My right to say "No."

But I lived through it. I survived it. And I got to reclaim—and redefine– everything he stole.

BUT DID YOU DIE?

The more that I opened up to my teacher, Mrs. Brown, the more I found myself sharing things that I didn't share with other adults, like my mistakes.

Because my mother would go off whenever I did even the slightest thing wrong, I didn't feel that I was allowed to mess up. I blamed myself when I knew I could have done better or made different decisions when the truth was, I'd never been taught how to do anything. Being an unparented, unprotected teenager meant that I had to learn life on my own. I'd never felt safe, and most of my choices reflected that. I needed to survive so that's how I moved, with survival in mind.

By the time I met Mrs. Brown in high school, I felt like I was in the streets more than I was at home. In the way that only she could, she began to teach me life lessons about accountability, forced me to think about the consequences of my choices, and in one particular conversation, she also gave me a masterclass in resilience.

I was telling Mrs. Brown that I was having a tough time. Instead of allowing me to either beat myself up about it or try to feel sorry for myself, she came hard as she always did.

She let me talk and then asked me a really unexpected question.

"Are you dead?"

I had no idea where she was going with that, but I decided to follow along to see.

"No," I said.

"And if you're not dead, then what happens? You get to do what?"

"I get to live another day."

"And what else?"

"I get to make better decisions tomorrow."

Once again, Mrs. Brown walked me right up to my personal power, introduced us, and made me shake her hand.

From that day forward, death became my bar. I decided that no matter how hard my life got or what happened to me, if it didn't kill me, that meant I had another chance. Those words became my life mantra.

Whether I am coaching myself or someone else through a tough time, I channel my inner Mrs. Brown and ask myself: "But did you die?"

If I'm not bleeding, in the hospital, or dead, then it's not that bad. I can still pull myself out of it. There is always tomorrow and tomorrow, I can make a different decision and figure something else out.

Fighting was nothing new for me. I was used to it. That is what living my life with this mentality felt like, another fight, except this wasn't a person. I redirected all of the energy I was putting into fighting other people into fighting for myself and me and my family's future.

Death is the lowest bar. Death means it's over. Otherwise, nothing can stop me.

As a young, single mother, I did what I had to do. I had to survive, keep a roof over my head, and feed my kids.

I am not scratching and surviving in the streets anymore, but the same rule applies.

Back then I may have been defaulting on payday loans that I couldn't afford to repay. Today it's taking big business risks that haven't always worked out the way I planned. Those decisions are on opposite ends of the spectrum, but the motive behind my moves is always the same. With any decision that I make, good or bad, I accept responsibility for the potential outcome.

Abused? I didn't die.

Business hit a bump in the road and didn't generate the revenue we projected? I didn't die.

Someone I loved betrayed me or left my life? I didn't die.

If I'm not dead, then what happens? I get to live another day. *We* get to live another day.

I know when we hear cliché statements such as "What doesn't kill you will make you stronger," we want to scream. It sounds like bullshit, like a cop out for the person who hurt you. It sounds like empty words that someone who hasn't really been through anything hard say.

You don't want to be strong. You want not to have been hurt. You want what happened to you to never have happened at all.

You don't want to be strong. You want sympathy. You want to erase the past. You want someone to pay for the pain they've caused you.

Strength is not what you wanted—not like this. Not at the expense of your body, your mind, and your heart. Not at the expense of your sense of safety and your self-esteem.

I know strength is not what you wanted. But it's what you got.

What could have killed you—physically, mentally, emotionally, and spiritually—*didn't*. You were not supposed to get back up. You weren't supposed to be able to believe that better was possible. You weren't supposed to bounce back.

People like us—people who have been through a lot of life, people who have been hurt—can forget how strong we really are. We're not still here by accident. We're here by intention. Getting back up when life knocks you down is a choice.

You get to get back up. You get to move on. You get to keep trying.

Undeniably, some bad things have happened to you. You can't change that. But you can decide what to do from here.

Wallowing in trauma does nothing but delay the inevitable and that is life going on.

Is your life going on with you? Or are you just going to sit in this trash and let trauma take more from you than it already has?

I am not saying it's easy. I'm saying it's possible.

PUSH PAST YOUR PAST

The first step in untethering yourself from your past is to accept it. The second step is to let go of any shame that is associated with it.

Let me start this section with this:

You are not what happened to you.

Yes, some bad things may have happened to you. *Very bad*. But you didn't cause it. There was nothing that you could have done. And if you have made some bad choices that led to you getting hurt or making life harder for yourself because you didn't know any better, you're entitled to mess up. Sometimes you mess up once and learn. Sometimes, most of the time, it takes more than once.

Regardless of how life up to this point has played out for you, you are not damaged goods. You're living, and you're learning. Everything in life is about a lesson, and it will teach you something if you let it.

I don't know if I would be the woman I am without abuse. As incredibly hard as it was to heal through that and live with the residue that it left, what I know for sure is that I took some lessons from that time in my life that I would not have learned otherwise.

It's a part of my story and because of it, I am who I am—good, bad, and ugly. I accept everything that has happened to me, and I use that acceptance to my advantage. I am unbreakable.

To redefine is to reframe how we look at things that have happened.

What if your trauma was a tool to teach you how to define your life? What if you can take that trauma, the lessons that it taught you, and thrive?

Whatever you've been through is hard, but let's look at it from a different point of view. If you think trauma was pointless, think again. Because of it...

1. **You learned about yourself.** Tough times in our lives teach us valuable lessons. You have a lifelong reminder that you're a survivor. You can, or should, appreciate the person you became in the process.
2. **You learned about other people.** It's arguably unfair that we have to learn about what we want by experiencing what we don't want. But trauma can teach us who and how to trust. It can teach us how we want to be loved or not loved, how we need to set boundaries and exert ourselves and our power to define and express how we want to be treated. You understand dangerous cycles and patterns and, with support and healing, how to identify and not repeat them.

Yes, they were hard-won, but all of these lessons are gifts—especially perspective.

Putting your past in perspective is life-changing. One of the most valuable life skills you can learn is how to compartmentalize. To not allow life to linger and to hold you down or back. To understand that one experience, one decision, one phase of your life doesn't define who you are forever. What happened to you, whatever it is, is a part of your life, not a life sentence.

Whether it's a fucked-up past or your present is rocky, you need to be able to put it in perspective.

When I am feeling shitty about something that has happened, here is my personal bounce-back checklist that helps to put it in perspective:

- **Is there something that I can do about it? (No, I can't change what happened. Next.)**
- **Does it define who I am? Does this affect who I am? (No, this is not the totality of my life, who I am, or what I've done).**
- **Does it change the person I want to be? (Absolutely not.)**
- **Can I move through it? (Can I still keep going? Yes.)**
- **Do I still have purpose? (Absolutely yes).**
- **Do I still have things that I want to do? (For sure.)**
- **Does this affect my current situation? What does this have to do with today? (This may be a setback, but I can come back.)**

Take this and apply it in your own life. As bad as whatever has happened may seem, it doesn't change who you are. It doesn't define you, and it doesn't end your life. You can still choose to make some different decisions. You can still live. You can transform. You can become anything you want.

Take what seems life-ending and make it life-changing.

BUILDING YOUR RESILIENCE MUSCLE

Resilience isn't some magic trick that only a chosen few can pull off. It's a skill and like any other skill, you can strengthen it with practice. So let's talk about some tools and techniques you can start using today to flex your resilience muscle and bounce back from whatever life throws your way.

1. **Flip the script on your thoughts:** When you catch yourself drowning in a sea of negative self-talk, it's time to flip the script. Instead of telling yourself, "I can't handle this shit," try, "This is tough as hell, but I've overcome some serious crap before, and I can do it again."
2. **Take care of yourself (for real):** Self-care isn't some fluffy, optional extra. It's a nonnegotiable necessity. Make time for the things that make you feel good in your body, mind, and soul. Hit the gym, meditate, journal your heart out, go forest-bathing (yeah, that's a thing), or whatever else lights you up. You can't pour from an empty cup, so fill yours up first.
3. **Set some damn boundaries:** My favorite line right now is, "The Answer is... NO!" Learning to say no, speaking up for what you need, and protecting your energy are all key ingredients in the resilience recipe. Start small and practice setting boundaries in your daily life. It might feel awkward at first but trust me, it gets easier with practice.

THE MESSY, BEAUTIFUL JOURNEY OF HEALING

I'm not gonna sugarcoat it: Healing is rarely a straight line from pain to peace. It's more like a wild, unpredictable roller coaster with twists, turns, and loop-the-loops. You might feel like you're making progress one day and slipping backward the next. You might have moments where you feel like you're right back at square one.

Guess what? That's totally normal. Setbacks, triggers, and shitty days are all part of the deal. The key is to keep putting one foot in front of the other, even when it feels like you're trudging through quicksand. Remember, progress isn't always a straight arrow, and every tiny step counts.

Be patient and kind with yourself. Talk to yourself like you would a bestie who's going through it. Celebrate the hell out of your wins, no matter how small, and don't beat yourself up when you stumble. This healing thing is a journey, not a destination.

TURNING YOUR PAIN INTO PURPOSE

When you're neck-deep in trauma and its aftermath, it's hard to imagine anything good coming out of that steaming pile of shit. But here's the thing: The human spirit is resilient. It has this incredible capacity for growth, even in the darkest, most painful moments.

There's even a fancy term for it: Post-traumatic growth. It's the idea that people can experience positive change and transformation as a result of wrestling with some seriously tough life stuff. This growth can show up in all kinds of ways such as a deeper appreciation for life, stronger relationships, a badass sense of personal strength, new priorities or life paths, and a greater sense of meaning and purpose.

Now let me be clear: This doesn't mean that trauma is some kind of gift or that anyone should go looking for it. And it definitely doesn't happen automagically or for everyone. But for a lot of people, the process of healing from trauma can also be a catalyst for some mind-blowing growth and change.

As you navigate your own healing odyssey, try to keep your mind open to the possibilities for growth and transformation. Ask yourself what lessons your experiences might be trying to teach you, what new perspectives they might offer, and how you can use your pain as rocket fuel for purpose.

Remember your trauma is a chapter in your story, but it doesn't have to be the whole damn book. With time, support, and a fierce commitment to your own healing, you can come out the other side not just surviving but thriving like a boss. You have the power to alchemize your wounds into wisdom and your pain into purpose. Keep putting one foot in front of the other, you brave, resilient badass. You've got this.

With *allllll* that said, I have one more thing to say to you:

PUBLIC SERVICE ANNOUNCEMENT: GET THE THERAPY YOU NEED

As a mental health professional and someone who has been through therapy, you need it. Therapy is an essential part of your healing journey. I know it's scary. I know it can feel one-sided and pointless in the process. But I promise you that the right therapist can be a lifeline.

If you've tried therapy before and hated it, or if you've been too afraid to try yet, I want you to change your mind. Literally.

You need professional help to unpack your past, process your emotions, and to help you see yourself, your past, and your future differently. Therapy and counseling can help you develop the tools to support positive change in your life, navigate setbacks, and keep life moving. Books like this one are amazing, and so are personal development courses and programs and life coaches. But you need someone, a good therapist or counselor, a trained professional, who you can reach out and touch and talk to. You don't have to do this alone.

Get the help you need to become who you want to be.

Alright, now that that's out the way it's time to put this resilience stuff into action. Let's dive into an exercise that's going to help you flex your resilience muscle and bounce back like a boss.

CHAPTER FIVE SELF-ASSESSMENT: RESILIENCE BOOTCAMP

Grab your journal or a piece of paper, and let's do this.

1. Think back to a time when life threw you a curveball and you knocked it out of the park. A time when you faced some serious shit and came out the other side stronger. Maybe it was a breakup, a job loss, a health crisis, or some other shitstorm. Write that down.
2. Now get real with yourself. What qualities, strengths, or skills did you tap into to get through that tough time? Did you get creative with problem-solving? Did you reach out for support? Did you dig deep and find a level of grit and determination you didn't know you had? Write down at least three badass qualities you showed up with.
3. Next, think about how you can channel those same qualities to deal with whatever challenges you're facing right now. How can you apply that same creativity, resourcefulness, or tenacity to your current situation? Brainstorm a few specific ways you can put those resilience muscles to work.
4. Now let's talk self-care. When the shit hits the fan, it's more important than ever to take care of yourself. What are three non-negotiable, self-care practices you can commit to no matter what? Maybe it's a daily walk, a weekly bubble bath, or a monthly massage. Write 'em down and put 'em in your calendar like they're VIP meetings with Beyoncé herself.

5. Finally, let's create a resilience mantra—a short, powerful phrase you can repeat to yourself when the going gets tough. It could be something such as, "I am resilient as fuck," "I've survived 100% of my worst days," or "I am stronger than my challenges." Choose a mantra that resonates with you and write it down somewhere you'll see it often.

Alright, you resilient badass, you've got your resilience toolkit loaded and locked. You've got evidence of your own strength, a plan to channel it, self-care nonnegotiables, and a mantra to keep you motivated.

But here's the thing: Resilience isn't a one-and-done kind of deal. It's a muscle you've got to keep flexing. So commit to doing this exercise regularly. Check in with yourself. Celebrate your wins. Adjust your plan when you need to.

Remember, you are a fucking survivor. You've got what it takes to bounce back from whatever life hurls your way. Keep showing up for yourself, keep putting one foot in front of the other, and keep reminding yourself of how far you've already come.

You've got this. Now go out there and show the world what resilience looks like.

6

RADICAL RESPONSIBILITY

"No, you don't have to do anything you don't want to do."

I was sitting with Mrs. Brown, my 10th-grade world history teacher and self-nominated mentor in her classroom one late afternoon as we talked about life.

I am not exactly sure how we got on the topic but the fact that we were was classic Mrs. Brown. We would start out talking about one thing, usually something that happened in school, and that would eventually lead to something—or everything—else.

I never knew where Mrs. Brown would take a conversation, but I could always count on her to give me something to think about at the end of whatever time we spent together. I never had a conversation with her where I didn't get a life lesson, although I didn't recognize how valuable her words of wisdom were until I was good and grown.

By the time I met her, I'd been through court-mandated counseling and group therapy and blah, blah, blah—all the things and professional people who tried to help me turn my wild adolescent life and nonchalant attitude around. But none of them could get through to me.

Mrs. Brown was different. Maybe because when I looked at her, I saw eyes that I could recognize. A Black woman who could have been a mother or a grandmother to me. She had a way of saying things that just stuck with me. Through her advice and guidance, Mrs. Brown changed my life in so many ways. She was one of the first people I could trust and confide in. She didn't judge me. She heard me. She *saw* me. I may have only known her for two years, but I will carry her with me for the rest of my life.

We'd been having after-school talks like the one we were having that day for some time, so I'd started to get used to how direct Mrs. Brown was. This woman did not beat around the bush at all. She taught me that you could be a straight shooter and not mince your words with someone and still care. I learned from her how to give tough love and truth, even with kids.

She taught me that there was only one person who had true control over my life, and that was me.

With everything that I'd seen and heard, it wasn't easy to rattle me. Mrs. Brown had managed to catch me off guard with this response. I was in semi-shock. I tried not to let my face show it.

"So I could just sit here and pee on myself?" I repeated what she'd said back to her to make sure I'd heard her correctly.

"Yes, you could."

Mrs. Brown and I were having a conversation about the things that we had to do and didn't have to do in life. She explained to me that, contrary to my belief, I didn't have to do anything I didn't want to do. I always had a choice with everything, regardless of who told me to do it or if it seemed like the right thing to do.

Being the smartass that I was, I challenged her.

Even from my limited point of view which of course, in my adolescent arrogance, I didn't realize how short-sighted it was and how little I actually knew, I realized that there were plenty of things in life that had to be done. Like getting up and using the toilet when I needed to.

"You have to go to the bathroom," I said defiantly.

"No, you don't."

I thought, *"Is this woman crazy?"* She had to be. I just sat there in silence. Mrs. Brown didn't flinch. She sat there too, listening as she always did, giving me an opportunity to put my argument on the table and speak my mind.

"If I don't get up and go to the bathroom, I will pee on myself."

"Then pee on yourself. What do you think happened before toilets existed? Peeing is a normal body function. It will happen whether you decide to put your pee in the toilet or not."

Mrs. Brown had said some remarkable things to me before, but this took the cake. This woman had literally just blown my mind. She continued to drive home her point.

"You don't have to get up and go to the bathroom. You *get to decide* to go to the bathroom," she continued, not batting an eye. "You don't have to do anything you don't want to do."

And that's how a story about peeing in my pants taught me everything I ever needed to know about personal responsibility and the power of choice.

THIS IS YOUR LIFE. OWN IT.

I am sure we can agree that if we're physically able, getting up and going to the bathroom is something we're going to do. But Mrs. Brown's point is as valid for you as it was for me: This is your life. You get to choose what you do—or don't.

Contrary to our own beliefs, we have more control over our lives than we've convinced ourselves that we do. Every day, we have choices to make. We get to decide what happens next.

We may not like the decision that we make. It may not feel good. It may hurt or disappoint some people. It may look different from what you've seen before. It may go against everything that the good, responsible human being that you've been taught to be should do.

But that doesn't change the facts. The choices you're making, whatever they are, are yours. Nobody else's.

Redefining ourselves means taking radical responsibility for our lives and everything that happens in it.

You are in control—always and in all the ways.

Two questions that drive my life and every decision I make are: What do I need to do to make sure that I am the boss of me? How do I ensure that there's nobody controlling my life?

I know it seems hard to believe, but I haven't felt controlled since I was a teenager. Out of survival, I had to become responsible for myself and others early, first my siblings and then my children. Outside of the little time that I'd spend with my grandparents, I never felt protected or cared for. My father was in prison, and my mother struggled with so many of her own issues that there was nothing for her to give me. If there was, she chose not to, so I was on my own.

That's not to say that I didn't or haven't had help in my life. I have, and a lot of it. But there is a big difference between someone helping you and someone handing you something. Nothing was handed to me, and that gave me a strong sense of self-accountability.

I refused to be anywhere I didn't want to be or that I decided wasn't good for me. I decided to always be in charge of *me*. And I've never changed my mind.

There are some people who will refuse to accept that you have this type of control. They would argue that there is always someone above you, pulling the strings of your life, calling the shots, telling you what to do, when to do it, how to do it, and who to do it with.

But is that really true?

You may have a boss or a manager on your job, but you can leave that job at any time.

You may be in school, but you don't have to go to those classes.

You may be married, but you can walk away from that relationship and never return.

The choice may be hard, uncomfortable, and unconventional. But the choice is still yours. If you decide to stay or not, that's up to you.

Let's stop using other people and what they want or want you to do as an excuse. You are responsible for yourself.

Now we're all adults here, so let me add this disclaimer: Our choices do have consequences. If you do decide to leave that whack job or flunk out of class without a Plan B, understand what that means. Be careful out there.

Now back to our program.

My point is this: Your life. Your decisions. You are liable for *your* actions.

If you commit a crime with a group of people and the police find out you were involved and come knocking on your door, they are going to ask you what you did. You'll be punished for the part you played.

If you're a Christian and you believe that someday Jesus is coming back to snatch believers to take them to Heaven, then you believe that you'll get there and be asked to be accountable for your actions and your life.

Whether it's prison or the pearly gates, you have to answer for you.

Nobody cares about what happened to you when you were 10 years old. Nobody cares about what your mom and dad did or didn't do. Nobody cares that your husband didn't love you or your friends.

They care about you—your actions, your choices. That's all that matters. Everything else is an excuse.

Take radical responsibility for your life. No excuses. No blaming anyone else. No accepting this as they are.

If you want something else, you have to make it happen.

THE ONLY OPINION THAT COUNTS IS YOURS

You have to define yourself by who you want to be and make decisions about your life based on what you want. That's it.

Your life is a personal decision. Who you are or are not. Who you become or don't. How you live, where you live, what you do for a living. What your marriage or relationship looks like and how you raise your kids. All of that is a personal choice.

Everyone you know has an opinion about what you should do with your life. But is this your life or theirs? You're not here to live out anyone else's dreams or finish their unlived life. Broken people who haven't done what they should with their own lives love to tell other people what to do with theirs.

You are here to live the life that you want to live, whatever that looks like.

Once my business became successful, it was clear to everyone I knew that my financial situation had changed for the better. If you were close to me, I openly shared my success. I was proud of myself and more than anything, I wanted to be an inspiration to other people. I felt that if I could do what I'd done, they could too. I started to get opinions from well-meaning people about what I should do with my money. So many people tried to tell me that I should buy a house. Why? Because that is what people "with money" are "supposed" to do.

I had the money to buy anything I wanted, including a house. I could have lived in any house in any neighborhood that I chose. But I didn't feel that home ownership was the best move for me yet. So I kept renting until I decided I wanted to purchase a home. When the time felt right for my family and me, I found the home I wanted us to have and bought it.

Where and how I lived didn't have to make sense to anybody else but me. Other people's decisions, opinions, and ideas don't matter to me.

I am the master of my life. I decide how life gets to go for me. And you do too for yourself.

YOUR CIRCUMSTANCES ARE NOT YOUR CHOICES

If you can make choices, you can make your life better or worse.

If this feels like news or a reminder to you, chances are you've confused your circumstances with your choices. It's easy to look around at our lives and convince ourselves that what we're sitting in is a result of circumstances beyond our control. But the truth is, our circumstances don't define us. What we choose to do with and about those circumstances do.

It's not where you are, it's where you can be.

Your race, your age, your address, your gender, or your sexuality does not define you. Your DNA doesn't define you. Your decisions from yesterday don't define you either. What defines you is what you want today and what you decide to do about it.

If you need proof of what's possible (Hint: We always do.), I'd like to offer you Exhibit A for consideration. Or maybe I should say Exhibit M. *ME*.

I am a Black woman from what is considered the hood. I had two hands-off parents. I wasn't parented or raised. I was sexually abused. I had six children by the age of 28. I barely graduated high school. Literally. I had all Ds and as fate would have it, my grandmother died of pancreatic cancer days before I was supposed to walk across the stage. My foster mother and my grandfather managed to get me a plane ticket from California to New York for the funeral. Mrs. Brown drove me to the airport. I went straight to the burial and back to the airport, where she picked me up hours before the graduation ceremony. When I say I barely made it, that's God's honest truth.

What in that story would have told you that my kids and I have never been homeless or hungry? What in that story would have told you that I would have not one but two college degrees and a top-tier industry certification? What in that story would tell you that I would run a million-dollar company that I built on my back?

None of that would have happened if I didn't make choices that led me there.

I am proof that you are in charge of your life. You can wake up tomorrow and be different. This is your story. You get to choose how it ends.

You have what you decide to go get it. You become who you decide to be—no more, no less. No one or nothing gets to define or choose for you.

You have the power to completely change anything. You are one decision away from a better life. If you only make one decision today, let it be this one: Don't relinquish responsibility over your life to anyone else.

THE REAL DEAL ABOUT RESPONSIBILITY

Now when I say take radical responsibility for your life, I'm not trying to hit you with some oversimplified, "Just do it" bullshit. I know life is messy, and there's a lot of shit that can get in the way of your choices and dreams.

Maybe you're dealing with some systemic fuckery or injustice that makes certain paths a hell of a lot harder. Maybe you've been through some trauma or setbacks that have left you feeling like you've got no control. I feel you. That shit is real, and it matters.

But here's the thing: Acknowledging that stuff doesn't mean rolling over and letting it win. It doesn't mean throwing up your hands and saying, "Well, I guess this is just the way it is." It means looking that shit dead in the eye, understanding how it's shaped your life, and then deciding how you're going to clap back.

Taking radical responsibility isn't about beating yourself up for everything that's happened to you. It's about owning your power to choose what happens next. It's about saying, "Alright, this is where I'm starting from. Now, what the hell am I going to do about it?"

WHEN SHIT GETS REAL

I'm not here to blow smoke up your ass. Taking radical responsibility is a lifelong hustle, and it's not always going to be a cakewalk. You're going to hit some roadblocks and detours along the way. There will be times when you slip back into those old, fucked-up ways of thinking or get caught up in what everyone else thinks you should be doing.

That's okay. It's part of the journey. The key is to catch yourself when it happens and get back on your grind.

When you find yourself playing the victim or making excuses, take a beat and ask yourself: "Is this how I want to show up? Is this getting me closer to the life I want?"

Then make a conscious choice to get back in alignment with your values and vision.

Surround yourself with people who have your back and hold you accountable. Create routines and habits that keep you anchored in your commitment to yourself. Most importantly, be fucking kind to yourself. Give yourself some grace when you stumble, and celebrate yourself when you get back up.

REDEFINING YOURSELF THROUGH RESPONSIBILITY

At the end of the day, taking radical responsibility is about taking back your power to redefine yourself and your life. It's about saying "fuck you" to the labels, limitations, and expectations that others have put on you and deciding for your damn self who you want to be.

When you fully own your choices, you open up a whole new world of possibilities. You start to see that you're not stuck with the life you have. You have the power to create the life you want. You begin to understand that your past doesn't get to dictate your future, and your circumstances don't define your worth.

REDEFINED

Taking radical responsibility is the key to unlocking your potential for transformation. It's the foundation you need to build a life that is authentic, fulfilling, and unapologetically fucking yours.

So start small. Start with one choice, one decision to honor your truth. And then build from there. With each intentional action, you'll be strengthening your responsibility muscle and paving the way for radical redefinition.

It won't always be comfortable. It won't always be easy. But damn, it will be worth it because on the other side of radical responsibility is a life that is truly, magnificently yours. And that, my friend, is what you're here for.

So let's get to work. It's time to get real with yourself. You've read this chapter, you've felt the fire in your belly, and now it's time to do something about it. This is your wake-up call, your rallying cry, your motherfucking call to action.

It's time to stop making excuses, stop playing small, and stop waiting for someone else to save you or hand you the life you want. It's time to take radical responsibility for your life and everything in it.

I know it's not easy. I know it can be scary as hell to own your power and make bold choices. But you know what's scarier? Waking up one day and realizing that you've let your entire fucking life pass you by because you were too afraid to take control.

You are not here to be a passive observer in your own life. You are not here to let your circumstances or your past dictate your future. You are here to be the boss, the master, the fucking CEO of your own existence.

So starting today, I want you to make a promise to yourself, a promise to start making choices that align with your values and your vision. A promise to start owning your power and your potential. A promise to start living like the badass, unstoppable force of nature that you are.

And I want you to imagine what your life could look like if you truly, radically took responsibility for it. Imagine the kind of relationships you could create, the kind of work you could do, the kind of impact you could make. Imagine the kind of person you could become, someone who is authentic, empowered, and unapologetically themselves.

That life, that version of you, is available to you. But you've got to choose it. You've got to fight for it. You've got to take radical responsibility for making it happen.

So what do you say? Are you ready to take control of your life and start redefining yourself on your own terms? Are you ready to stop making excuses and start making moves? Are you ready to look your fears, your doubts, and your limiting beliefs dead in the eye and say, "Not today. I'm in charge now."?

If you're ready–truly, gut-level ready -- then let's do this damn thing. Let's take radical responsibility and create the life you were born to live.

The journey starts now, and it starts with you. So take a deep breath, square your shoulders, and let's fucking go. You've got this. I believe in you. Now it's time for you to believe in yourself and take radical responsibility for your life.

Let's redefine what's possible, one bold, intentional choice at a time.

CHAPTER SIX SELF-ASSESSMENT: OWNING YOUR POWER

This self-assessment is designed to help you reflect on how well you're taking radical responsibility for your life. Answer each question honestly, and use your responses to identify areas where you can start owning your power more fully.

1. On a scale of 1-10, how much do you believe that you have the power to change your life through your choices? (1 = not at all, 10 = completely)

2. In what areas of your life do you feel most in control and responsible for your outcomes? (e.g., career, relationships, health, etc.)
3. In what areas of your life do you feel least in control and responsible for your outcomes?
4. How often do you blame external factors (e.g., other people, circumstances, etc.) for the things you're unhappy with in your life?
   a. Always
   b. Often
   c. Sometimes
   d. Rarely
   e. Never
5. When faced with a challenge or problem, how likely are you to take action to address it, rather than avoiding or complaining about it?
   a. Very likely
   b. Somewhat likely
   c. Neither likely nor unlikely
   d. Somewhat unlikely
   e. Very unlikely
6. How often do you make choices that align with your values and the life you want to create, even when it's uncomfortable or scary?
   a. Always
   b. Often
   c. Sometimes
   d. Rarely
   e. Never
7. On a scale of 1-10, how much do you trust yourself to make good choices for your life? (1 = not at all, 10 = completely)
8. What is one area of your life where you know you need to take more radical responsibility?

9. What is one bold choice you can make today to start owning your power in that area?
10. What is one limiting belief or fear that might be holding you back from fully taking radical responsibility for your life?

Scoring

For questions 1 and 7, a higher score indicates a stronger sense of personal power and responsibility.

For question 4, "Rarely" or "Never" indicates a higher level of radical responsibility.

For questions 5 and 6, "Very likely" or "Always" indicates a higher level of radical responsibility.

Reflection

Review your responses and reflect on what they reveal about your current level of radical responsibility. Celebrate the areas where you're already owning your power, and identify the areas where you have room to grow.

Remember, taking radical responsibility is a journey, not a destination. Use this self-assessment as a starting point to get honest with yourself, and commit to taking bold, aligned action to create the life you want.

You have the power to redefine what's possible for your life. It all starts with owning your choices, one day at a time.

RADICAL RESPONSIBILITY

This exercise is designed to help you reflect on where you might be giving your power away, and how you can start owning your choices and creating the life you want.

Part 1: Reflect on Your Choices

Think about an area of your life where you feel stuck, unfulfilled, or like you're not living up to your potential. It could be your career, your relationships, your health, or anything else.

Now, take a hard, honest look at how you might be contributing to the situation. What choices have you been making (or not making) that are keeping you stuck? Write them down.

Next, consider how you might be blaming external factors for your situation. Are you telling yourself that it's someone else's fault, or that circumstances beyond your control are holding you back? Write down those excuses.

Now, look at what you've written. How can you reframe those choices and excuses to take radical responsibility? What would it look like to own your power in this situation, and start making choices that align with the life you want?

Part 2: Make a Bold Choice

Based on your reflection, identify one bold choice you can make today to start taking radical responsibility in this area of your life. It could be saying no to something that doesn't serve you, setting a boundary, or taking a step towards a goal you've been putting off.

Write down your choice, and why it matters to you. What will making this choice help you create or become?

Now, identify any fears, doubts, or limiting beliefs that might be holding you back from making this choice. Write them down.

For each fear, doubt, or limiting belief, write down a reframe or a truth that counters it. For example, if your fear is "I'm not good enough," you could reframe it as "I am capable and worthy of creating the life I want."

Finally, take your bold choice and break it down into one small, concrete action you can take today. Write it down, and commit to taking that action, no matter what.

Part 3: Reflection

After taking your bold action, take a moment to reflect. How did it feel to own your choice and take radical responsibility, even in a small way?

What did you learn about yourself and your power to create change?

How can you continue to apply the principle of radical responsibility to other areas of your life?

Remember, taking radical responsibility is a practice, not a one-time event. The more you flex this muscle, the stronger it will become, and the more empowered you'll feel to create the life you truly want.

So keep coming back to this exercise, keep owning your choices, and keep redefining what's possible for your life. You've got this.

7

REDEFINING YOUR RELATIONSHIPS

REDEFINING YOURSELF HAS TO INCLUDE REDEFINING YOUR RELATIONSHIPS. It means reevaluating the people in your life, picking the people you want and need in your life, and pruning and purging the people you don't. It means deciding what relationships look like for you, regardless of how unconventional they are. It means determining how you need others to show up in your life, and it all starts with understanding what you want and need as a measuring stick for what you want and need from everyone else.

Trauma can take you in one of two ways. For some, being traumatized makes it impossible to trust anyone, including yourself. So there is a struggle to assert and protect yourself in the world.

When abuse and abandonment are a part of your life story, it feels so familiar there is a tendency to recreate it in relationships instead of avoiding it. These are people who find it hard to speak up for themselves and give away far more than they receive.

And then there's the opposite: Those who vow never to allow anyone to take advantage of them ever again.

At 14 years old, I discovered that end of the spectrum, and I never looked back.

The man who molested me took my innocence and body but gave me my voice. With no parents to protect me, I accepted early in life that I needed to protect myself.

Once I met people like my teacher Mrs. Brown and my good friend in high school who knew what was happening to me at home, I was reminded that I had a say in everything about my life. A beast was fully unleashed. I became the no-nonsense person that I am today.

I understood that I had the power to decide for myself what I wanted to happen to me.

I learned how to create boundaries and nonnegotiables for how I live my life and how the people who I allow into my life are required to treat me.

This is my voice, and you will listen. This is my body, and you will not touch any parts of it that I don't allow. This is what I am offering you, and you will only take what I give you, nothing more. This is my life, and I will live it the way I choose.

These are my boundaries—and you will honor and respect them.

This approach to life sounds rigid, and I will be the first to admit it is. As I've gotten older and wiser, I've learned to share and deliver my boundaries differently, depending on the scenario, versus vomiting them all over people as soon as I say "Hello." But I never compromise them.

Once I drew my line in the sand and made it clear where I stood, I lost some people in my life, and I know I'll lose lots more. But I know my boundaries help me more than harm me. Here's how:

I feel in control of myself and my life. My boundaries give me a sense of safety. I don't feel like I am in the world wondering how I will respond to situations as they come. I know what I am doing and what I am not. My boundaries are always my baseline. My "No" is my "No."

I'm never confused about what opportunities to take and what friends to make. Whenever I have a chance to do something new in life or in my business, or when I meet new people, I bounce them against my boundaries first. It's easy for me to determine if I belong there or if I should consider allowing someone in my life.

I can be myself. If it makes me uncomfortable or I don't like something, and the only reason I am considering it is because it's fun or it's what somebody else wants me to do, I don't do it. I don't like the taste of liquor, so I don't drink. I don't like certain foods or certain places, so I don't eat those foods or go to those places.

It doesn't matter to me who else is doing it. It doesn't matter who else may try to pressure me to do it. I don't have to be anything other than who I want to be. I don't have to do anything other than what I want to do.

I trust my own opinion. The first person I consult is always myself. Do I ask questions when I don't know something? Yes. Do I seek out wisdom and expertise from people who have been where I am trying to go? Yes. Do I ever release responsibility for myself and my life to anyone else? Absolutely not. When it comes to making decisions, I ask myself questions such as, "How do I feel about this?" "How will this affect me and my life?" "Does this honor me?" and "Does this feel good and right for me?" If I can't see how whatever I am considering is good for me, I don't do it. Period.

I don't feel compromised and taken advantage of in my relationships. My boundaries ensure that I don't feel like I have to be someone I am not or give more than what I have to give. People in my life know where I stand and that violating me in any way is not an option. If someone I care about asks me to do something with or for them, my number one question is, "Is there a way that I can honor the person who is asking this of me without dishonoring myself?" When the answer is "No," I don't do it, and I don't feel guilty about it.

My voice is the loudest in my head. I think any fucks about what people thought about me left me at 12 years old. I don't allow what other people think to override what I think.

I took a flag, wrote my boundaries on it, and I planted it. I always stand in who I am and what I want for myself. Now it's time for you to do the same.

You've struggled to find your way, your voice, your respect, and your people in this world because you've never planted your flag.

You've always gone along to get along. You have been far more concerned with what other people think versus how you feel about yourself. You're scared to tell people where you stand, what you will and won't do, what you want, and what you will tolerate.

It's time for you to finally plant that flag.

It's time to stop impersonating someone else's identity out of fear that no one will like you and be able to be your person. It's time for you to be so clear about who you are that regardless of who comes into your life and what they want or need from you, you have your boundaries in place, and you can decide what to do. If you decide to support someone, you do it because you want to, not out of fear. If someone gets something from you, it will be because you gave it to them, not because they took it from you.

It's time to know who can come into your life and who needs to leave. It's time to teach people how to treat you.

When we feel frustrated, disrespected, or taken advantage of, we often want to point the finger at the other person. But in actuality, it's not their fault. It's ours. When our boundaries are tested, pushed, or broken, we have no one to blame but ourselves. It doesn't matter if it's our children, our boss, or anyone else. They are a mirror, reflecting back to you who you are as a person and what you've allowed and accepted.

If I am the person who teaches people how to treat me, then why am I unhappy that I am not being treated well? If someone yells at me and I feel belittled, at what point did I say (either verbally or by accepting the behavior) that it was okay for them to speak to me that way?

If I feel bad about how my children are talking to me then that means at some point, I let them know it was okay to speak to me in that way. If my manager disregards my schedule and constantly calls me on weekends, it's because I've allowed that to be.

The question is not why they are doing it. The question is, "Why are you allowing it?" Ask yourself, "What do I need to change in this situation?" If you don't know the answer to that question, let me help.

You need boundaries.

When you write your own textbook for your relationships and interactions with anyone in your life, personal or professional, it becomes easier to teach people how to treat you.

CHAPTER SEVEN SELF-ASSESSMENT: SETTING YOUR NONNEGOTIABLES

Boundary setting begins with you knowing what your nonnegotiables are. This is who you are, what you stand for, and the truth that you want to walk in and that you want other people to see. Your nonnegotiables set the stage for what you will tolerate and what you won't. These are the lyrics to your life song and your chance to stand in and declare your power. Here are mine again:

This is my voice—and you will listen.

This is my body—and you will not touch any parts of it that I don't allow.

This is what I am offering you, and you will only take what I give you— nothing more.

This is my life—and I will live it the way I choose.

These are my boundaries—and you will honor and respect them.

Now it's your turn. Think about these questions:

- What does respect look like to you?
- How do you want to feel as it pertains to the relationships in your life?
- What makes you feel angry? Frustrated? Unappreciated? Not valued? How can you avoid feeling that way again?
- In what scenarios in your life have you felt that you gave too much of yourself and resented it? What would you have done differently?

Once you've answered these questions, reverse engineer your thoughts into nonnegotiable statements. For example:

- I will not tolerate disrespect of any kind.
- I will not be pressured into doing anything that I don't want to do.
- I will not remain in relationships that make me feel bad about myself.

Feel free to borrow my set of nonnegotiables, too.

YOUR RELATIONSHIP RULES

Now that you have your baseline for your boundaries and your nonnegotiables, let's take it a step further. You're going to create your relationship rules. These are your boundaries in action and what people can expect from you—always. Think about yourself like a new iPhone. When people get you, they know they can expect your rules, just like they can expect a charger cable.

To give you a feel for what relationship rules can look like, here is my list:

Expect honesty. Know that I'm always going to be honest with you. This one has cost me some people. Initially, people are attracted to my strength, conviction, and how no-nonsense I am. They think they like how I'll always tell them the truth, if they ask me.

Here's the thing about that: The truth is always invited until it's time for it to sit down at your table. But I stay true—to myself and others—at all times.

Don't waste my time. I am an open book when someone asks me for advice. But my wisdom comes with a price. If you ask me for a solution to a problem, I'm now invested. When I see you suffering, I take on your emotion. I feel bad and I want you to improve your situation, whatever it is. That means that if I show you a way out and you don't take action, I'm pissed. If you refuse to move and you would rather lose, then I'm going to leave. I can't sit back and watch people volunteer to stay in situations that are harmful to them. Action is the price you pay for my advice.

After realizing that not everyone who asks is ready to do what's required, I've had to learn when to be a listening ear and when to actually share my opinion. I've learned to compartmentalize people.

Translation: I won't be involved in your day-to-day, but I will love you from a distance.

Don't mess with my family. Self-explanatory.

When I meet new people or come into a new situation or environment, I set my boundaries quickly, and I don't flinch. If you want to be in my life, there are rules. Take them or leave me.

CHAPTER SEVEN SELF-ASSESSMENT: SETTING YOUR RELATIONSHIP RULES

Now it's your turn. Think about these questions:

- When you think about the true you, who is that?
- What do you want people to know about you and how you move in the world?

- What can people always expect from you?

Once you've answered these questions, reverse engineer your responses into a relationship rule. For example:

- I'll always tell my truth, even when it hurts me or someone else.

Between your nonnegotiables and your relationship rules, you now have a clear set of requirements to define how you run relationships. You know how you show up for yourself and other people, and how you expect people to show up for you.

Your boundaries are as much for you as they are for others. When you can be clear about who you are, what you want and what you need, you give others the opportunity to decide if they will be that person for you. Maybe they can or maybe they can't. Your boundaries are in place to ensure you won't have to compromise yourself to keep anyone or anything.

Your boundaries list may evolve and grow as you do. Revisit it. And most importantly, live it.

YOU'RE GOING TO PISS SOME PEOPLE OFF

If you started to see some relationships flash before your eyes as you were working through your boundaries, good. The people who you think you are going to lose by putting boundaries in place shouldn't have been in your life in the first place.

There are a lot of people who only want to be in your life for what they can get from you, not what they can—or should—give. There are people who love the idea of you being weak, willing to yield to the pressure of their opinions and feeling okay with being disrespected and deprioritizing yourself.

Your choice to choose yourself may hurt some people. Correction: It *will* hurt some people. It will piss people off. But here's the question: Would you rather it be them or you?

This is your life. Telling your truth—and living it out—is for you. The person you want to become and the things you are setting out to do are not about proving anything to anyone.

Now let's admit that it does feel good when you are nothing like the "theys" from your past said you would be. But you don't have to show and tell. They'll see and know.

You don't have to be preoccupied with having something to prove. This is about you becoming better and not bitter. This is about you, your best self, and your best life. Why?

Because you may not get the recognition you deserve. There will be people who will never acknowledge your wins. There will be people who will never accept how they played you or how they hurt you. They will never admit how they discounted and disappointed you. And that's okay.

Whatever you decide to do, whoever you decide to become next for better or worse, do it for you.

When I decided to write this book, all I could think about was how my story and sharing my truth would affect other people. For the first time in my adult life, I was scared.

I was scared about what everyone in my family, especially my mother, would think about it. I come from a family that is a lot of things. We're far from perfect, but what we don't do is tell each other's secrets. Speaking publicly about my sexual abuse and that my mother knew what happened to me made me uncomfortable.

On a positive note, I saw this book as an opportunity to share my story to inspire people.

I wanted to be a voice for people who couldn't believe in themselves and who'd never had anyone in their corner before. I wanted to help as many people as I could. And all of that is still true.

But as I thought more about who this book was for, I realized that before it could be about anyone else, it had to be for me.

My goal, first and foremost, was to say everything I wanted to say. This book is about healing for me before it's about hurting my family or helping anyone else. I decided that I couldn't–or wouldn't–censor myself for anyone else. Doing that would defeat the purpose of the honesty I stand for.

Your bold moves may break hearts, and so will your truth. As writer Ann Lamont says, "You own everything that happened to you. Tell your stories. If people wanted you to write warmly about them, they should have behaved better."

I couldn't have said it better myself.

Your truth is your truth. If redefining yourself means releasing your truth, whatever that looks like, then do it. But I caution you to do it for you with noexpectations of getting anything in return except your freedom.

PSA: You may never get the apology you deserve.

I understand that validation is an important part of the recovery process for any type of trauma or hurt. I understand that it's important to you and you want it badly.

I also know that it's not required.

You want the person or people who hurt you to acknowledge and apologize for what they did. You've been waiting. You may be waiting for the rest of your life–and you do not have the rest of your life to wait.

Sometimes (let's be real, most of the time), you will have to give yourself closure.

The person who abused you or inflicted pain on you that led to trauma likely does not have the emotional maturity, capacity, or skillset to understand the depth of what they did to you.

Even if they know what they did to you was wrong, to admit it to you they would have to admit it to themselves. Some people in your life aren't willing or able to do that.

You've done your work to heal yourself or you are in the process of doing it. To be able to give you the apology you deserve, the person who hurt you has to do their work.

I lived 30-plus years of my life waiting for my mother to acknowledge that her boyfriend abused me. She hasn't done that, and neither has anyone else in my family.

She had children with this man, my siblings, so to acknowledge what happened to me would change our entire family dynamic. My mother is still very much in love with him and obviously, my brothers and sisters love their father. She still wants them to be a family. To acknowledge my abuse and apologize to me would mean she would have to trade her fantasy of their family for my truth. That will never happen.

My mother has to live with the fact that someone molested her daughter and she knew it. She allowed it to happen. She is living with that and I am living my life.

I've released any hope of ever receiving the acknowledgment and apology for what happened to me. Not only did my mother not believe me, but she created a story that I had an affair with her boyfriend, which means that I accept my family's blame for what happened. I carried all of that, and I still do.

I could put my life and growth on pause indefinitely and wait for something that could never happen, or I could accept my truth as enough, choose myself, and let my life provide the lessons I need to learn to become the woman I need to be.

Some people come into our lives to teach us what to do. Others teach us what not to do. Both are necessary. Take what you've been taught and redefine.

REDEFINING ROLES IN YOUR LIFE

We all have fantasies and ideals of what we think certain relationships in our lives will look like. Girls grow up thinking they know what a husband should do, and boys have a vision of what they want in a wife.

We have an image of what we think a mother or father should be. We imagine what we will be like as partners, parents, and employees in jobs we can't wait to run to in the morning because fantasies are always perfect, right?

With everything we watch on television, see in movies, on social media, or from the outside looking in on somebody else's real life, we all have models for roles in relationships.

Like a writer developing her script, we take our lives, put ourselves in the lead role, and assign roles to our supporting characters. Everybody has a part and place, complete with words that should be said. It sounds good in our minds.

Except this is real life, not your favorite soap opera or sitcom. These models of identities and ideals are bullshit.

Shaping our identities based on what we think we or anyone else should be is dangerous. These expectations will hold you hostage. They don't leave room for you to be you, for others to be them, or to create a relationship that allows everyone to peacefully coexist, provided that your boundaries are respected.

Can you be positively influenced by how you see someone else show up in a role in their lives? Sure. And you should be. But if you attach to that ideal, you won't allow yourself to determine what that role needs to look like for you.

Once I learned and accepted this and redefined the relationships that needed to change, I changed too. For the better.

Let's talk about them...specifically those who show up in your life consistently.

Myself

I'll start with the most important relationship I have: The one with myself.

The LaKeysha I am today is far from the LaKeysha I used to be. I am different in so many ways, and not just in age but in how I act and view the world and the people in it.

I thought girls who grew up like me, who had grades like me and families like mine, were destined to be stuck right where they were. I didn't think they could create lives they loved. I thought they had to be hard and unfeeling in order to survive in this world.

I've redefined myself from a standoffish, noncaring individual to an open-minded, empathetic woman to a woman who isn't just successful in terms of the money in her bank account, degrees on her wall, and cars in her driveway but a woman with the things that can't be bought. These are things that have to be earned such as becoming a woman who is highly aware of herself, a woman who can pat herself on the back and celebrate herself, a woman who can honor herself, a woman who can love.

I am someone who I never thought I would or could be, someone who didn't have role models or a roadmap to teach me how to do anything but who figured it out. Redefining starts with self, and I am living proof.

Marriage

When my now husband, Randall, and I had just met, his mother came to visit. As we sat in our small kitchen, she grilled me lightly, as good mothers tend to do.

"Do you like sports?" she asked.

Most women wouldn't have thought twice about lying to her to be liked. Not me.

I didn't hesitate. "No, I don't."

"Well, you better start. This is a sports family, and Randall loves sports."

"Yeah. No. He'll be watching sports by himself."

My soon-to-be mother-in-law clutched her proverbial pearls at my audacity. "What?"

I stood my ground. "I don't like sports. They're not interesting to me."

And that conversation set the tone for the rest of my marriage.

Fast forward, Randall and I have been married for more than 20 years. We didn't make it this far by forcing ourselves to become one person. Instead, we remained separate people who could be responsible for ourselves and each other. He has opinions, and I have mine.

We didn't try to force the other to yield to the identity of the other person. We sat down and talked about our beliefs about marriage and family. We found the commonalities, and that became the basis of our relationship, not outdated models of what marriage is supposed to look like.

I am who I am, and he is who is, and those two people love each other. I am not going to stop doing the things that I like because my husband doesn't enjoy those things, and vice versa.

We're not married for life. We're married for as long as we work and for as long as we're willing to do the work to make it. We don't worry about years. We could be together for 30, 40, or 50 years. The number doesn't matter. What does matter is we choose each other today.

Our Redefined Rules for Marriage

1. We define marriage for us and no one else. We decide what marriage looks like for us. Our relationship. Our rules.
2. We have a TV in every room in our house.

3. When it comes to sports, I am there for the food and the team colors.
4. We are committed to our individuality—and each other.
5. We try to love each other in the way the other wants and needs to be loved. That has been a ride all in itself.

My husband had a very traditional two-parent family, and that was his model for being a husband and a father. There are aspects of his mindset that I love and appreciate—his sense of stability, loyalty, and devotion to our kids and me.

And then you have me—someone who didn't grow up with two parents loving each other and who never thought I would get married. I honestly believe that marriage is a social construct that has brainwashed people into thinking marriage is the epitome of love when it's really about how much income tax you pay and that monogamy can be selfish.

So, needless to say, I had to learn how to love and be loved.

The first time that I experienced Tony Robbins—the world-famous, no-bullshit coach and speaker live—my life changed. During the multi-day conference, we got into our limiting beliefs, and it was deep. Like *deep, deep,* and so much more than I'd expected. It was probably one of the first times that I was so open and vulnerable with myself and, in a room full of strangers, allowed myself to really feel my feelings without talking myself out of my emotions under the guise of being strong.

I realized that I still was carrying so much from my childhood. I had acquired all of these things—the house, the cars, the businesses, the family, the ability to spend thousands of dollars to be in the room I was in— but deep down, I still felt like that little girl from the hood. The first thing that came out of my mouth when someone asked me about myself was that I had been sexually abused and abandoned. That was my story, and I was sticking to it.

On the surface, I was successful. But I realized that I didn't feel like enough. I didn't believe I deserved the lifestyle I lived. I didn't deserve kids who were so loving to me. And I didn't deserve my husband.

I came home from the conference and apologized to him. For 18 years, I'd allowed my trauma to represent me far more often than the healed version of myself that he deserved. I'd put him in a box and tried to define for him how he needed to love me and dictated what our relationship should be.

He grew that box, but there were times when I fought to keep him, and us, in it. Whenever he didn't do something exactly how I wanted it, I threatened to walk away. That was fear and was so unfair to him. I had my boundaries, but that didn't mean that I had to box in someone whose only intention was to love me.

I decided to be more open and to accept him for who he wanted to be, just like he'd done for me, and not the person that I decided he had to be in order to love me.

And that, my friends, is love redefined.

Motherhood

As a grown woman, I had to accept two things:

1. My mother will never be the mother I want or needed her to be.
2. The mother that I got to see was not the mother I had to be.

For me to be able to communicate with my mother, save my sanity, have any sense of peace, and have some version of a relationship with her, I had to release my expectations of what a mother is supposed to be. She doesn't choose or protect me. She is not nurturing. She doesn't give me loving advice to help me discern between right and wrong. She is literally the person who gave birth to me.

But, ironically, I learned a lot from her, even if it was what *not* to do.

My relationship with my mother taught me how to redefine motherhood for myself. I had to decide how I would mother my own children. From the moment I found out I was pregnant with my first baby, I decided that I was going to parent differently.

I knew I never wanted them to be hungry or to worry about where they would sleep. I didn't always have millions in the bank, but I kept a roof over my kids' heads, and they were fed. I've given them the best life I can.

I wanted my children to always feel protected. I didn't want to beat them, and I didn't want them to fear me. I wanted them to respect me. I do have rules, but I am far more open than my mother was. They are minors and need some boundaries. Trust me, we have our fair share of "Who-the-fuck-do-you-think-you're-talking-to?" moments in my house. I discipline them, but I also talk to them.

We have in-depth conversations where I am always asking them questions about what they think. Instead of always telling them what to do, I guide them to think about why they did something and assess the consequences of their actions. I want to help them learn how to think for themselves, self-manage, self-regulate, and adjust their behavior when they need to.

I let them make decisions about their lives. I am here to help my kids, not to do their work for them. One of my favorite questions to ask them is, "What do you need from me to be the best version of yourself?"

I can give them information and inspiration, but I can't give them their identity. I can give them experiences and extra help when they need something beyond what their father or I can give them, like tutoring, but I can't give them success. They have to earn that on their own.

I tell them that there are only three things they have to do in this world: You're born, you're here to procreate—obviously you can control that, but naturally, it can happen without you doing anything about it—and then you die. What you do in the middle of that is your business.

I make it clear the lives they're living are theirs, and they have to take responsibility for them.

I wanted to be able to tell them I loved them. I love on my children all the time. I want them to know they're loved and that they will always have someone in their corner, someone who hears and believes them. That is what motherhood looks like to me.

My Redefined Motherhood Rules

1. My kids are themselves, and I am me. We don't force each other to be something we are not.
2. My children will never doubt my love for them. There is nothing they can do to make me take my love away from them.
3. I don't have to be perfect to be a good mother.
4. I will not lose my identity to be a mother.

I give myself permission to also be the mother I feel my children need, and that may not look like the textbook image of what the world thinks a mother should look like. Because of that, I question my mothering all the time.

I wonder if I am giving my kids enough of what they need. Am I still a good mother, even though I can't be at every college football game? Am I scarring them for life by not making it work to have dinner with them every night?

When I feel guilty about the sacrifices I have to make to give my kids a better life, I bring myself back to the reality that I shouldn't feel guilty at all.

I can't mother or be a wife every second of every day, and my husband and my kids understand that theoretically, but it doesn't mean I don't disappoint them when I can't (or sometimes don't want to) be where they need me to be.

Redefining motherhood meant that I had to learn the difference between my family's priorities and mine when I am not in mom mode. I can't be pressured by other people's priorities, including the people I love the most. I've had to learn to live with that.

Once I decided that I was going to do whatever I needed to do to give my kids a better life than I had, I also accepted the sacrifices that come with my decision.

My parenting style doesn't have to look like any other mother's. I had these kids, and what I say goes for our family. I am passing that permission slip on to you: You can be the mother or parent that you want to be.

Let this also be a reminder that the mother you had is not the mother you have to be.

God gave your babies to you so you could rewrite your story and write a new one for them. Create the family you want, whatever that looks like.

Mentoring/Teaching

Never in a million years did I think I would be a teacher of any kind or work with children. If I could have chosen any profession for myself, I can assure you that would not have been it.

I was still in foster care when I graduated from high school and started college, and that meant I could practically go to school for free with financial aid. I was taking classes and passing them, but I had no idea where I was going in terms of a job. What I did know was I needed something that paid me enough to take care of myself and my six-month-old baby.

I asked an advisor for the easiest possible path to the two things that mattered most to me, a degree and money.

When she told me that with a degree in early childhood education, I could pretty much write my own ticket career-wise, I was sold. And the rest is history.

One of my first teaching jobs was at an all-girls school in Southern California. With no formal teaching experience, I was thrown into a

REDEFINING YOUR RELATIONSHIPS

classroom full of teenage girls who had all been expelled from their previous schools for behavior.

In every one of their faces, I could see myself at their age.

They were girls from the hood who were assumed to be no good, and they lived up to their reputation. They had the same nonchalant attitude. No sense of accountability. No one to believe in them anymore. Their only goal was to survive. This school was their last resort before society and the system gave up on them.

The classroom was rowdy, and it was clear that the last thing any of the girls wanted to do was be there and listen to me. I had no idea how to teach them, but I knew I could figure it out. But first, I had to set some ground rules:

Rule #1: You can do what you are supposed to do or not. It's your choice.

Rule #2: You will do what you're asked to do first and then ask questions or express how you feel about it. You have a right to your opinion and your feelings, but you lose the right to share them if you are defiant and noncompliant.

Rule #3: I am absolutely about life. If you put your hands on me, I am fighting you back. No questions asked.

Now that I know the law, Rule #3 is questionable, but it was exactly how I felt then. To be honest, I would probably say the same thing today. What I needed them to know right away was that I was different from any teacher they'd ever met.

I didn't judge them. I didn't bring a bunch of ridiculous rules with me. I recognized where I was and what those girls needed. I brought what Mrs. Brown had taught me and what I'd proven to be true with my own life as soon as I learned it: You get to decide what you want to do with your life.

For the first time, I introduced them to exactly what I'd been given at that age—the gifts of personal power and perspective.

I gave them permission to choose for themselves and offered them an opportunity to try a new way of doing things. I made it clear that their experience with me and their education could be drastically different if they were willing to make different decisions.

The choice was theirs.

Some of them got it, and some didn't. That's the life of a teacher. I may not have been able to transform every girl's life in the room in the few weeks I was there, but I influenced where and how I could.

I didn't know it then, but that experience helped to shape how I work with people today. Whether I am working with clients as a behavioral therapist or mentoring business owners as a CEO coach, I approach it the same as I did in that classroom.

I make it clear that I am different from anyone else they've ever met. I'm direct. I'm honest. I'll call you out on your shit. And I lay down the rules early.

Typically, I've been some version of them at some point in my life. Hard headed. Counted out. Confused. So I know what needs to happen to get to the other side of struggling and being stuck.

Some may say it's too bold of a statement, but I know it to be true: Listen to me, and I will change your life.

When it comes to changing anything—your mindset, your beliefs, your habits, or your behaviors—listening more than talking at the beginning of your process is a necessity.

If you knew it all, you wouldn't be here. Admit when you know what you don't know.

Before you pop off about why something won't or can't work for you, try it first. Be open. A closed mind can't change.

If you are willing to open your mind to a new way of thinking and get the right people around you as guides in your life to help push you forward, you'd be amazed at how drastically your life can change.

CHAPTER SEVEN SELF-ASSESSMENT: REDEFINING ROLES

You may have specific roles and relationships in your life that need to be redefined.

What you saw growing up, peeping over the fence and looking at other people's lives, or what you see on social media, may not work for you, and that's okay. Throw away the idea of what a relationship is "supposed" to be and redefine it based on who you are, who they are, and what you need that relationship to be.

Let's begin to reevaluate your relationships. Get a sheet of paper and write down all of the important people in your life and their relationship to you. Think through these questions:

- Which of these relationships, if any, feel difficult to you? Why?
- What would you like each of these relationships to look like?
- What expectations are you holding those people to that they've proven they are unable to meet?
- Where have you built that relationship based on what you thought it should be and not what you want or need it to be?

If the rules of these relationships need to change, these are conversations that you'll need to have.

REDEFINE THEN REBUILD YOUR CIRCLE

Redefining your relationships may mean leaving some people behind. You may not need to toss every relationship you have in the trash. But you do need to reevaluate them to determine who to keep in your circle and who you need to show to the door.

Take your list from the redefining roles exercise. Are these the people you spend the most time with? If anyone is missing from the list, add them.

On a separate sheet of paper, make three columns:

Column 1: Keep. These are the people who are healthy for you to keep in your circle.

Column 2: Toss. These are the people who need to go.

Column 3: Compartmentalize. These are the people who you'd like to keep in your life, but you choose not to be a part of their day-to-day lives.

Now you have to decide who goes in what column. Here are questions to help you:

- Does this person respect my boundaries and my nonnegotiables?
- Is there reciprocity in the relationship?
- Can I be myself with this person?
- Will this person allow me to grow and redefine myself?

Your keep list is the people who check all of these boxes. These are people who want to see you shine and are here to help you become the best version of yourself.

Your toss list is those who check none of them or who can't check the boxes that are most important to you. Maintaining a relationship with these people will impede you from living your best life.

Your compartmentalized list is the people who may check some of those boxes but there is some misalignment in how you and that person think or choose to live your lives. You need to limit your interaction with them for your own mental safety and sanity.

Before we move on, let me say this: You will have feelings about letting people go. You'll feel guilty for leaving people you love behind. It's normal. Feel it. Grieve it. But don't let those feelings or those people convince you to let them stay when you know it's time for them to go.

WHAT'S KEEPING YOU FROM THE NEW PEOPLE YOU NEED

The work that you did to redefine and reevaluate your relationships may have left you with some voids. You may have realized that you need more people around you who can give you the support, guidance, and room you need to change.

Like any other change in our lives, changing the people around us and letting new people into our lives can be hard. We have to fight the resistance and, let's be real, the fear that comes up. Stop believing the lies we tell ourselves when we're afraid to get to know new people.

Allow me to call you out on a few of those lies that I know are swirling around in your head right now:

- **I can't trust anybody.** Not true. You can't trust people who've repeatedly hurt you, but you can trust people. Trust yourself to know what's good for you and to hold your boundaries.
- **They don't think how I think.** This is a popular one when we start to elevate and expand our lives. There are definitely people out there who are on the same path as you are. It's a big world, and you're used to being in small rooms. They exist. You just have to put effort into finding them.
- **They don't understand me.** Here's an idea: How about you tell them so they can understand?
- **They don't know me like my old friends, family, partner, etc.** That's true. But believe it or not, all things, including intimate relationships, have to start somewhere. Holding on to toxicity and trauma is an excuse.

NEW PEOPLE, NEW PLACES, NEW PERSPECTIVES

In high school, my teacher and mentor, Mrs. Brown, didn't just teach me. She opened doors for me to discover new parts of myself.

Back then, there was a program at our school called peer counseling that allowed trained students to be an ear for other students who may be experiencing mental health challenges and need someone to talk to. The program was a place where kids could come and have candid, confidential conversations about whatever they were going through—from grades to not being able to make friends and sometimes more serious issues such as abuse or suicide ideation.

Mrs. Brown was the school's peer counseling advisor, and she encouraged a friend and me to become counselors. We'd meet with other students after school. It was for credit so I figured, why the hell not?

I thought I would hate it. I was so closed off, and I wasn't open to meeting new people. I had two close friends. If I wasn't with them in class or at lunch, I was huddled up somewhere in a corner by myself.

Thankfully, I trusted Mrs. Brown and did it. Becoming a peer counselor changed the course of my life.

I learned a lot from those experiences, first and foremost that I wasn't alone. When you're a teenager who is dealing with as much shit as I was, you feel like you are the only one in the world with those issues. But I wasn't. I heard it all. And those conversations with other students really opened my eyes.

They had struggles, too, some similar to mine, some not, but they were problems that they had to work through. I talked to kids who also didn't want to get up and come to school. Even "smart" kids hated coming to class sometimes. Others didn't feel loved by their parents or boyfriends or girlfriends. Some needed the courage to have hard conversations with somebody who had hurt them or made them uncomfortable in some way.

These were people who were different from me, but we shared some of the same experiences. I got to put my Mrs. Brown hat on and share with other students some of the empowering wisdom that she shared with me.

And just like that, a behavioral therapist was born.

Of course, a lot happened before I could claim that title, but it was that experience that opened my eyes to who and what I could be. It felt easy for me to help other people work through their problems. Now I know that is a gift that I've honed over the years—a gift that I possibly never would have unwrapped had it not been for Mrs. Brown, who saw the potential in me and gave me an opportunity to use it and grow.

It is so important to have people in your life who can look past who you are and see the potential in who you can be.

When I was in my late 20s, my husband noticed that every winter, I would go into a depressive state. It was like I would do a 180. I'd go from loving and being open with him to being detached and constantly wanting to be by myself all the time.

On top of this, normal depression would set in. I had so much going on in my life. I had three small kids, two of them infant twins and one who had recurring respiratory issues that our doctors couldn't figure out. I was constantly calling out from work to take care of a sick baby and was one sick day away from losing my job. To say that I felt like I was losing my mind was an understatement.

Once I started to recognize what he pointed out to me, it scared me. I didn't like feeling that way, and I didn't know how to control or stop it. I knew I needed to talk to a professional about what I was going through. At that time, I really didn't believe counseling worked, at least not for me.

In foster care, I'd been to mandated therapy. I went through the motions half-heartedly because I had to. I never got anything significant out of it. But I was feeling desperate, so I decided to try again.

Until I met this new therapist, I'd only had therapists and counselors who would sit there and listen to me talk for 45 minutes without giving me any direction or insight at all. It always felt one-sided, so I thought that was what therapy was.

This new therapist was completely different. First, she let me talk, but she talked back. She challenged me with really hard questions and then gave me suggestions and solutions to help me get unstuck.

She was one of the first people to help me take a serious look at my behavior patterns and habits and figure out why I would find myself back in the same place in my life over and over again. Instead of allowing me to run from myself and wallow, she helped me to reframe my thoughts and behaviors so they weren't debilitating anymore. She heard my limiting beliefs and helped me to knock them down one by one.

With everything that was going on, I'd dropped out of school. My new therapist encouraged me to go back and really push myself. She saw and told me how smart and capable I was. She helped me to see that school wasn't something that had to be hard for me, a story that I'd told myself all my life. It wasn't that I couldn't succeed in school, I just needed to apply myself, understand how I learned, and work with my weaknesses instead of against them.

That woman helped me to move forward. That's really an understatement. She saved my life because she was able to get me to change my perspective and see myself and my life differently.

You will only grow to the level of the people around you.

According to psychologist David McClelland, the people you associate with determine 95 percent of your success and failure in life. So when it comes to the people around you, you have to choose wisely. As you build your new circle, here are some people you need to keep close:

People who can see your potential. We all need someone in our lives who can see us as more than what we are and as more than we can see ourselves. These are people who will look at your life and find your greatness to prove to you why you can do something rather than pointing out all of your flaws as proof of why you can't. This is also the person who will push you when you need it most.

People who can change your perspective. These are people who can help you see life through a different lens. They walk and talk differently. They live differently. They challenge your thinking. You see something in them that you want to embody and you use them as a tangible example of what's possible for you.

People who can take you places. You need people who can open doors for you, literally and figuratively. You need people who can get you in rooms and help you to expand your world by introducing you to new people and spaces.

People who can be powerful for you when you can't yet. Sometimes when you don't have the confidence to do something on your own, you need someone who has the faith that you don't yet. These people will allow you to borrow their beliefs if you need to. Standing next to strength can be a substitute for your own.

NAVIGATING THE SHIT SHOW OF SETTING BOUNDARIES

Alright, let's cut the crap. Setting boundaries is not for the weak-minded or the people-pleasers. It's one thing to know you need to set them, but actually growing a pair and doing it? That's a whole different level of badassery.

When you start putting up those "Do not cross" signs in your relationships, you might face some serious pushback, both from the people around you and from that scared little voice in your own head. You might worry about being abandoned, being labeled as a selfish bitch, or struggle with the urge to keep everyone happy at your own expense.

This shit is normal, but it doesn't have to hold you back from demanding the respect and space you deserve in your relationships. Here's how you can navigate this minefield:

1. **Start small:** If the thought of asserting your boundaries has you shitting bricks, start with baby steps. Practice saying no to small requests or setting a boundary with someone you trust. Build up that muscle.
2. **Change your fucking perspective:** Setting boundaries isn't selfish. It's the ultimate form of self-love and self-respect. You're not responsible for managing other people's reactions to your boundaries. You're responsible for honoring your own damn needs and values.
3. **Get ready for some discomfort:** Setting boundaries is going to feel about as comfortable as a cactus up your ass at first, especially if you're not used to it. Expect and accept this discomfort as part of the process. It doesn't mean you're doing it wrong.
4. **Have a ride-or-die crew:** Surround yourself with people who will cheer you on and have your back as you put up those boundaries. They can give you a reality check, be your emotional bodyguards, and hold you accountable to your badass new standards.

Remember, setting boundaries is a skill and like any skill, it takes practice. Be patient and kind to yourself as you stumble through this new territory.

FEELING THE FUCKING FEELINGS WHEN YOU LET SHIT GO

As you redefine your relationships, you might realize you need to kick some people to the curb, even people you love. This can unleash a shitstorm of grief and loss, even when you know deep down it's what you need to do for your own growth and sanity.

You've got to let yourself feel those feelings, no matter how much they suck. Grieve the loss of the relationship you wanted, the potential you saw, the memories you made. Let yourself be fucking sad, angry, and heartbroken. This part of the process is not optional.

But as you're ugly-crying into your pillow, try to remember what you're gaining by letting go. You're making room for relationships that truly honor and support the badass that you are. You're claiming your right to be treated like the fucking boss that you are. You're freeing up your energy to pour into your own growth and into people who actually deserve you.

As you grieve, be extra fucking gentle with yourself. Wrap yourself up in support and self-care like a warm, fuzzy blanket. And keep reminding yourself why you're putting yourself through this torture— not to punish yourself, but to create a life and relationships that make you feel alive.

IT'S TIME TO REDEFINE YOUR FUCKING RELATIONSHIPS LIKE THE BOSS YOU ARE

Alright, we've been through some shit together here. You've seen that redefining your relationships isn't a nice-to-have, it's a must-fucking-have if you want to redefine yourself. You've got tools for setting boundaries, facing fears, and dealing with the inevitable feelings. You know what green flags to look for in ride-or-die, level-up relationships.

Now it's time to take this shit and run with it. It's time to get real as fuck about which relationships are lifting you up and which ones are dragging you down. It's time to start having those gut-wrenching but game-changing conversations. It's time to start setting those boundaries and meaning business about them.

I'm not going to sugarcoat it: This work is about as easy and comfortable as squeezing lemon juice into a paper cut. It demands courage, discomfort, and a willingness to let people down in the short-term to honor yourself in the long-term. But holy shit, is it worth it.

Imagine what your life could look like if you were surrounded by people who truly see you, respect the hell out of you, and push you to be your best self. Imagine the freedom and power you'd feel if you weren't constantly bending over backwards to meet someone else's bullshit expectations. Imagine the mind-blowing depth of love and support you could experience if you cleared out the energy vampires to make space for soul-level connections.

That life is yours for the taking. But you've got to be willing to reach out and grab it. You've got to be willing to redefine your relationships on your own fucking terms, no apologies.

So take a deep breath, channel your inner badass, and take the first step. Set that first boundary. Have that first come-to-Jesus conversation. Cut the cord on that first toxic relationship. And then keep fucking going.

You've got this. You're worth it. And on the other side of this gauntlet is a relationship glow-up beyond your wildest dreams. So let's fucking get it.

Part II
REDEFINING YOUR LIFE

8

THE REDEFINING PROCESS

The first part of this book was about getting to the root of who you are.

If you've done the work, you've peeled back the layers of your life and increased your insight into why you are the way you are and why you show up. Before we move on, let's recap what you've explored so far:

- Your worthiness and a reminder that you deserve good things and to live a good life, whatever that looks like for you.
- Your definition of life and success and how you've likely determined who you should be based on other people's expectations of you.
- Your need to get really honest with yourself about who you are and what you want.
- Your resilience and how the tough times you've experienced in your life have made you stronger than you knew.

- Your relationships as you've started to reevaluate the people in your life, who you may need to release, and how to redesign the relationships that remain.
- Your need to take radical responsibility for your life and everything that happens in it.
- Your resistance to change and why you've hit walls that kept you stuck whenever you've tried to do something different.

If you made it this far, I want to say something to you that you probably don't hear often enough: I'm proud of you.

I am proud of you for pushing through what is hard, then and now. For opening yourself up to new possibilities. For taking a hard look at yourself, your life, and your circumstances, and deciding that you will commit to yourself and commit to becoming the person you were born to be on your own terms.

I hope you are proud of yourself too. Now, let's go further.

In this second part of the book, we'll dive into what it takes for you to create any change in your life and redefine your behavior so you can redefine your life.

Are you ready? Let's go.

DON'T MAKE YOUR FIRST MOVE WITHOUT KNOWING YOUR NEXT

You know by now how much my teacher, Mrs. Brown, taught me about life. From her, I learned so many big lessons that I didn't have the big words to describe them.

Being the wild child I was before I met Mrs. Brown, I didn't think before I did anything. If I wanted to do it, I did it. I didn't think about any consequences of my actions or accountability to myself or other people. I was driven by emotions and my need to survive and get what I needed at the moment.

Mrs. Brown changed that for me. She taught me the value of slowing down and planning. I learned everything I did should have a reason. I learned I should think for myself and be clear on what I was doing and why. She taught me how to move from impulsiveness to intention.

I know that I am nobody's employee. I've always known that. But I've also always known that inconsistent income wasn't an option for me. I've been on my own longer than I was taken care of by an adult. I've always had responsibility, and a lot of it. As tempted as I've been to walk away from jobs I've had over the years, I never have. My plan has always been to take care of myself and my kids, so I knew making an impulsive decision could jeopardize that.

Plans can change, but you need to have another plan in place first.

Don't abandon a job and your only consistent paycheck because a boss pisses you off. Don't up and leave your city without a place to live and some way to feed yourself when you get there. It's not that you want to leave, it's how you leave. It's not wise to blow up your life and make your situation worse until you have a better plan.

Take it from me and Mrs. Brown: You don't make your first move without knowing your next move.

After transitioning from early childhood education to behavioral health, a whole new world of possibilities opened for me. Once I decided that I wanted to move into a new field, I went all in. I'd learned that I could create a career for myself that would allow me to provide the life I wanted for myself and my kids. The average hourly salary for new clinicians was between $45-$50 an hour, which was a lot of money for me at the time. That was great, but once you tell me there is potential for more, I want the most.

The more I learned, the more confident I became in my skills. I increased my salary requirements to above average. Still, I knew there was more for me.

I was working with a local ABA Company full-time and took a freelance position with a small practice, working directly beside the owner. There, I learned I was much more than a clinician. I took her client roster from 20 clients to more than 200 in a little over a year. I knew how to manage people and business, but I needed my clinical certification to become a master clinician and really start earning more.

That exam was standing in the way. I'd taken it several times and studied my ass off, but still failed. Each time I sat for the exam and saw that big "Fail" on the screen was more heart-wrenching. I wanted it more than anything.

A friend who owned several group homes suggested that I reach out to someone she knew who could help me pass the exam and also perhaps give me some tips on growing from a contractor to owning my practice. This woman was the head running her own behavioral health company by working with centers in California, and she could really be a great relationship to have.

I was resistant at first. I didn't know her, and I didn't want to know her either. But I followed my friend's advice. BIG Lesson: If you want to be successful, do what successful people tell you to do.

Once I met her, we clicked. I actually found that I liked her a lot. Not only did she help me pass the exam, but this woman also helped me build the business I have today. She gave me pointers on how to start my own behavioral health practice. She was an open book, teaching me the process of getting large clients and connecting me to the vendor process.

She opened the doors. All I had to do was walk through them. I started planning how I was going to start a new business quickly. I knew I needed help, so I picked up the phone and started asking. I started with a friend who was in HR.

"I have $250," I said. "What can I get for that?"

She consulted with me and helped me with our first new-hire training. She became my HR director, and she is still with me today.

I got another $250 and reached out to another friend who helped other new practices with credentialing and billing. With another

$250, I convinced an accountant to help me with my initial paperwork to get the business set up and to put me on a month-to-month contract to handle my finances.

Piece by piece, I assembled my own dream team—a group of women, each an expert in their respective field, who believed in me and what we were building. We ended that first year in business with $280,000 in revenue. Fast forward, I looked up and had a multi-million-dollar business.

And that's the story of how I flipped $750 into $1 million in revenue.

I didn't plan on achieving that much success that fast. One day, I was trying to make enough money to pay my bills and take my kids to Chuck E. Cheese on the weekend without having to sweat through my shirt worrying about how I was going to pay for pizza to being responsible for $700,000 in payroll a year. Not only did I have my own bills to pay but as a CEO, I was responsible for my team's bills too.

Talk about some scary shit!

But I did it. I am *doing* it. As I am writing this book, my company is on track to hit more than $7 million in revenue this year. A little girl from the hood who wasn't supposed to be anything who became *everything*.

In addition to a lot of hard work, a few key things happened to get me here.

1. Deciding that I needed to make as much money as I could.
2. Creating a plan to get from where I was to where I wanted to be.
3. Getting help to implement the plan, including finding an expert to tell me what I needed to do (and actually *listening*) and asking for help to fill in the gaps of what I couldn't do myself.
4. Keeping my head down and working the plan until I got to where I wanted to go.

I didn't set out to run a company. I made many stupid-ass mistakes and had plenty of what-the-F—am-I-doing moments. There were times when I had to choose between payroll and taxes and found myself with a tax bill that was double the original amount. My imposter syndrome kicked in and tried to convince me I had no business running a business and should stop pretending like I could. People had told me all my life that I couldn't do anything, had labeled me as lazy and a liar. There I was, with all this money and success showing up and feeling like I stole it and at any moment, somebody would walk up on me and take it because I didn't deserve it.

I had to work on worthiness, once I realized that was an issue. I had to expand from laboring to thinking, from being an employee to a CEO. The mindset work was harder than the business work. I had proof that I wasn't what my mind tried to convince me I was. It was a battle I was determined to win.

With all of that to conquer, I never abandoned my business, even when I messed up or got scared. I was always willing to ask for help when I needed it. I kept pushing and redefining my life.

Why? Because I had a plan. I knew I had to work that plan and get to where I wanted my life and company to be.

You may not want to start a company like I did. You may want to plan to lose 50 pounds, get a degree, or move to another state. Whatever you want to do, it won't magically happen. You have to get intentional.

This is how you make it happen.

STEP ONE: DECIDE YOU NEED TO DO SOMETHING DIFFERENT

As we've talked about throughout this book, nothing will change unless you want it to. You have to be fed up. You have to be uncomfortable and sick of your current situation. You have to want something different more than you want anything that will get in

THE REDEFINING PROCESS

the way of you having it—your comfort, other people's opinions, your money, whatever.

Alright, let's dive into the first step of redefining your life: Deciding that you need to do something different. This is where it all begins, where you draw a line in the sand and say, "Enough is enough. I'm ready for a change."

Listen, if you're not sick and tired of your current situation, if you're not at the point where you'd rather chew glass than spend one more day living the way you're living, then you're not ready. You've got to get to that place where your desire for change outweighs your fear of it.

Here's how you know you're there:

- You're done making excuses. You're done blaming your circumstances, your past, or other people for where you are. You're ready to take radical responsibility for your life.
- Your comfort zone feels like a prison. The things that used to pacify you—the Netflix binges, the retail therapy, the numbing out—they don't cut it anymore. You're ready for more.
- The opinions of others don't mean shit to you anymore. You're done living for your parents, your partner, your friends, or society's expectations. You're ready to live for you.
- You're willing to give up what you have for what you want. You're ready to let go of the good to make room for the great, even if it's scary as hell.

If you're nodding your head, if you're feeling that fire in your belly, then congratu-fucking-lations. You're ready for step one.

YOUR ACTION ITEMS:

1. Make a "Fed Up" list. Write down all the things you're sick and tired of in your life. Don't hold back. Get it all out on paper.
2. Pick your top three. Circle the three things on your list that you're most fed up with, the things that are causing you the most pain or frustration.
3. Get emotionally honest. For each of your top three, write down how it makes you feel. Dig deep here. Do you feel angry? Helpless? Scared? Resentful? Get in touch with those emotions.
4. Make a declaration. Write down a statement that sums up your commitment to change. Something like, "I am no longer available for a life that doesn't light me up. I am ready and willing to do whatever it takes to create the life I truly want."
5. Share your declaration. Tell a friend, a family member, or post it on social media. Make your commitment to change public. This will help hold you accountable and cement your resolve.

Remember that getting fed up is not about wallowing in negativity or self-pity. It's about using your discontent as fuel for transformation. It's about deciding that you're worthy of a better life and that you're willing to fight for it.

So embrace the discomfort. Lean into the frustration and use it to propel you forward into the next step of your journey. You've got this. Your redefined life is waiting for you. It all starts with deciding that you're fucking done settling for less than you deserve.

STEP TWO: FIGURE OUT WHAT THE HELL YOU ACTUALLY WANT

After committing to change, you need to know exactly what you want. This is bigger than wanting not to feel sad or frustrated anymore. You have to go deeper to discover.

Often we know how we feel, and that is a sign that something needs to change. Our lives are off. We know something or a lot of things aren't working, but we're not sure exactly what. We feel unfulfilled in some way, but we can't pinpoint why. We start with feeling unhappy, and it snowballs from there.

While feelings are a good indicator that something needs to change, especially if they are consistent, you may not know why you're feeling that way. You have to get to the root of your unhappiness. If you don't, you could end up chasing some goal and putting in all of the work to get there only to realize you're still not happy or satisfied.

You may think you need to lose 50 pounds to find a partner when you really need to work on your confidence—you should have that at any size—and find someone who loves you. If you are unhappy at work, you may not need to throw your career in the trash. It could be the job you're in.

Get to the root of what you are feeling so you can get the real answers you need.

Be honest. Don't be afraid to really dive into your life and your feelings. Have that heart-to-heart conversation with yourself. Revisit the work you did in chapters one, two, and three, where you got clear about yourself and the life you wanted. Be honest with yourself about where you are. That will help you determine where you want to be.

Visualize where you want to be. Imagine what your life would look like if you reached your goal. Envision what the other side looks like. How would you feel? What would you be doing? This will help you hone in on the right goals.

Visualize where you don't want to be. What is the worst thing that could happen if you stay where you are? If you look two years down the road and you haven't moved at all toward what you want, what will that look like? What about in five years? In 10? Play it all the way out for yourself. If you have a family of your own or you want one in the future, think about how your inaction will affect you and the people connected to you. What will it cost if you do nothing? What will you lose?

Focus on yourself. Your motivation should never be what other people want you to do, even as a parent. Your child's needs and wants are different. If you allow other people to dictate what you do, that will almost always lead to you betraying yourself. Don't worry about other people around you. Don't worry about how other people feel about you. If it's warranted, be respectful, responsible, and honest with the people you love. But always remember this is your life and you're the one who has to live it.

Get help. You may need someone, like a therapist, a life coach, or a mentor, depending on your goal, to help you work through this.

Here's the thing: A lot of us think we know what we want, but we're actually just chasing someone else's dream or trying to slap a band-aid on our deep-rooted unhappiness. We think a new job, a new relationship, or a new body will solve all our problems. If we don't get to the root of what's really driving our dissatisfaction, we'll end up right back where we started.

So how do you figure out what you really want? It's time to get honest as fuck with yourself.

YOUR ACTION ITEMS:

1. Get quiet and get real. Find a space where you can be alone with your thoughts without any distractions. Sit with yourself and start digging. What's really bothering you? What feels off in your life? What's missing?

2. Make a "Fuck Yes" list. Write down all the things that make you feel alive, excited, and fulfilled. What lights you up? What makes you lose track of time? What would you do even if you didn't get paid for it? These are the things you want more of in your life.
3. Make a "Fuck No" list. Now write down all the things that drain you, that feel heavy, that you dread. What are you tolerating in your life? What are you doing out of obligation or fear? These are the things you want to eliminate or minimize.
4. Visualize your ideal day. Get specific as hell. What time do you wake up? What does your morning routine look like? What kind of work are you doing? Who are you interacting with? How do you feel throughout the day? Write it all down in vivid detail.
5. Ask yourself the hard questions. What would you do if money was no object? What would you do if you knew you couldn't fail? What would you do if you only had a year left to live? These questions will help you cut through the noise and get to the heart of what really matters to you.
6. Get an outside perspective. Sometimes we're so close to our own bullshit that we can't see it clearly. This is where working with a therapist, coach, or mentor can be game-changing. They can help you identify blind spots, challenge your assumptions, and empower you to gain clarity on what you really want.

Remember, figuring out what you want is a process. It's not something you do once and then you're done. As you grow and evolve, your desires and priorities will too. The key is to stay curious, stay honest, and stay connected to what feels true for you.

And don't be afraid to want what you want, even if it doesn't make sense to anyone else. Your dreams are valid, your desires are worthy, and you don't need anyone's permission to go after them.

So get clear on what you want, and then get ready to make it happen. The world needs your unique brand of magic, and it all starts with knowing what the fuck you want.

STEP THREE: MAKE A PLAN

You're clear on what you want, but wanting something is not enough. Having the will to do something isn't enough either. Yes, you need both desire and internal motivation to move but bigger than that, you need a plan to get to where you want to go.

There are three specific questions you should ask yourself as you determine what plan of action will get you to your goals.

1. What will this take?

In behavioral science, we use an approach called a task analysis to break a big goal down into small steps to ensure that each step is accounted for.

If your goal was to make a pancake, you would:

- Pull out your ingredients.
- Measure your ingredients.
- Mix your dry ingredients together in a bowl.
- Add your wet ingredients.
- Preheat a frying pan.
- Add cooking spray to the pan.
- Pour your batter in for each pancake.
- Flip the pancakes.
- Remove the pancakes from the pan when both sides are brown.
- Repeat the pouring and flipping until you have the number of pancakes you want.

As detailed as that process may seem, if you skip one of those steps, your entire plan to have the breakfast you want falls apart.

That is how you have to approach the foundation of your life plan. You need to think through every step it will take to get you from where you are to where you want to be. No step is too small.

2. What choices do I have?

There is always more than one way to achieve a goal, and they all can work. The question is, can they work for you? Before you start ruling out all possibilities, let me say this—your discomfort is not a disqualifier. That means you may be scared to try something new or fear you might fail.

You may have never lifted a weight in your life, but you need to strength train to get to your goal weight. You may need $1,500 to start a business, and you don't have $0.15 in your bank account. Maybe you want to change your career and need a college-level math class, but you've never been good with numbers.

Doing any of these things may make you uncomfortable, but they are not impossible.

You can start with a lighter weight and build up your endurance. You can get a part-time job or borrow money. You can study math and get a tutor. All these things are within your reach.

You are only allowed to disqualify an option if it is impossible—not hard.

As you are evaluating your options to determine what can work for you, discomfort aside, determine what is impossible for you to do right now and rule those options out. Then choose a path based on what is available to you.

3. What do I need?

You will likely need to learn something new, so you'll have to determine what capabilities or skills you need.

4. Who do I need?

If your goal is big enough, you'll probably need someone to help you. People are a necessary part of your process. Here's why:

They can tell you what to do. Someone who has been where you are going can tell you how to get there. This could be a mentor or coach.

They can teach you what to do. If there is a skill you need to learn, there is someone who knows it and can teach it to you.

They can do it for you. There will be some things that you need to be done, but you don't need to do them. If you needed a house, you wouldn't likely learn how to pour concrete or hang the drywall. You would hire an expert to do that. If you pay or promise your way to hire help, do it.

Alright, you've gotten fed up, you've gotten clear on what you want. Now it's time to make a goddamn plan because let's be real, a goal without a plan is just a wish. And you're not here to wish for a better life, you're here to create one.

So how do you make a plan that actually works? It's time to get strategic as fuck.

YOUR ACTION ITEMS:

1. Break it down. Take your big, audacious goal and break it down into smaller, manageable steps. This is where a task analysis comes in clutch. Write down every single action you need to take to get from where you are to where you want to be. I mean every single one, no matter how small

THE REDEFINING PROCESS

or seemingly insignificant. The more detailed your plan, the better.

2. Identify your options. There's more than one way to skin a cat (sorry PETA), and there's more than one way to achieve your goals. Brainstorm all the different paths you could take. Could you take a course? Hire a coach? Find a mentor? Do it yourself? Write down every option you can think of.

3. Get uncomfortable. Here's the thing: The best option for you might also be the scariest. It might push you way out of your comfort zone. But growth and comfort rarely coexist. If an option scares the shit out of you but you know deep down it's the right move, don't disqualify it. Lean into the discomfort.

4. Be realistic. That being said, there's a difference between uncomfortable and impossible. If an option is truly out of reach for you right now—like you need a million dollars to start your business and you're currently living paycheck to paycheck—it's okay to cross it off the list. Focus on what's actually doable for you in this moment.

5. Identify your gaps. Look at your skills, your knowledge, your resources. What do you already have that you can leverage to achieve your goal? What do you still need to acquire or learn? Be honest about your gaps, and then make a plan to fill them.

6. Rally your squad. Listen, no one achieves anything great alone. You're going to need support, guidance, and expertise along the way. Make a list of the people you need in your corner. Who can mentor you? Who can teach you the skills you need? Who can handle the tasks that are outside your wheelhouse? Reach out to them and enlist their help.

7. Create a timeline. Take all the steps you've identified and plot them out on a timeline. What needs to happen first? What can happen concurrently? What's dependent

on something else being completed first? Give yourself deadlines for each milestone, and then hold yourself accountable to them.

Remember, a plan is not a promise. It's a living, breathing document that can and should be adjusted as you go. Don't be afraid to course-correct if something isn't working or if a better option presents itself. The key is to stay flexible, stay committed, and keep moving forward no matter what.

And if you get stuck, if you start to doubt yourself or your plan, go back to step one. Reconnect with why you're doing this in the first place. Remind yourself of what you're fed up with and what you're fighting for.

Here's the thing: You wouldn't have gotten this far if you didn't have what it takes to see it through. You are capable of so much more than you give yourself credit for. With a solid plan in place, you're unstoppable. So take a deep breath, roll up your sleeves, and let's get to work. Your redefined life is waiting for you, and it all starts with a fucking plan.

STEP FOUR: MODIFY YOUR BEHAVIOR

Getting to where you want to go means nothing if you don't know how to stay there. You have to make the change stick.

If you have tried to change anything in your life before, you probably have a pattern. You get fed up and fired up. You tell yourself this is it. You are going to do it this time. You start strong and before long, you find yourself right back where you started or in a worse position than you were.

You know from experience how hard it is to sustain success, even if you want something badly. Let me solve the mystery for you. It comes down to your behavior. You are setting yourself up for failure if you try snatching something out of your life without replacing it with something that your mind and body perceive to be just as good or better.

Changing anything in your life is a result of a series of behavior changes. As you set out to change, you have to look at what behaviors have been working for you that you can leverage. If you are disciplined, you'll need that. If you are a fast learner, you can bring that. Those habits work in your favor.

But there are some behaviors that have been holding you back, and those are the habits you want to get rid of. It's as simple as stopping them. You need to replace them.

Let's say you want to lose weight, and you need to stop eating sugar. If you take sugar out of your diet, you need a substitute behavior that makes you feel as good as sugar does. You need to know:

- How does eating sugar make you feel?
- What healthier alternative gives you the same feeling as eating sugar?

Here's another example: You like to share your life with friends, especially when you are setting out to do something new. You're used to picking up the phone and calling one particular person, but you know that relationship is not healthy for you. You need to know:

- How does talking to this person make me feel? Focus on the benefits.
- How can I make new friends I can call who understand me, can share my excitement, and are positive and healthy for me?

When you know what behaviors help and which ones hurt, and then replace the habits that hurt with healthier, productive ones, you'll start to see your changes actually stick.

CHANGE YOUR FUCKING HABITS

You've gotten fed up, gotten clear, and made a plan. Congrats, you're on your way. But now it's time for the real work to begin because here's the hard truth: You can have the best plan in the world but if you don't change your habits, you'll end up right back where you started.

Habits are the backbone of lasting change. They're what keep you going when motivation fades and willpower runs out. And if you want to redefine your life, you've got to redefine your habits.

So how do you do that? It's time to get real about what's working and what's not.

YOUR ACTION ITEMS:

1. Identify your current habits. Take a hard look at your daily routines and behaviors. What do you do automatically, without even thinking about it? What are your go-to coping mechanisms when you're stressed, bored, or upset? Write it all down, the good, the bad, and the ugly.
2. Evaluate what's working. Look at your list of current habits. Which ones are serving you? Which ones are aligned with your goals and values? Which ones make you feel good, energized, and proud? Circle those. Those are the habits you want to keep and strengthen.
3. Evaluate what's not working. Now look at the habits that are holding you back. Which ones are sabotaging your progress? Which ones leave you feeling drained, ashamed, or stuck? Which ones are you clinging to out of fear or familiarity, even though you know they're not good for you? Put a big fucking X next to those. Those are the habits you need to break.
4. Find your replacements. Here's the thing: You can't just eliminate a bad habit and expect it to stick. Nature abhors a vacuum, and so does your brain. If you take something

away, you've got to replace it with something else. For each habit you want to break, identify a new, healthier habit you can put in its place. If you want to stop stress-eating, what can you do instead when you're feeling anxious? If you want to stop procrastinating, what can you do to get yourself into action mode?
5. Start small. Habit change is hard. If you try to overhaul everything at once, you'll burn out faster than a cheap candle. So start small. Pick one habit to focus on at a time. Make the new behavior so easy and doable that you can't say no. Want to start exercising? Commit to doing 10 squats a day. Want to start meditating? Commit to one minute a day. Build from there.
6. Track your progress. What gets measured gets managed. Keep a habit tracker. Use a sticker chart or find an accountability buddy. Celebrate your wins, no matter how small. And if you slip up, which you will because you're human, don't beat yourself up. Just get back on track as quickly as possible.
7. Be patient. Habit change takes time. Studies show it can take anywhere from 18 to 254 days to form a new habit, depending on the behavior and the person. So don't get discouraged if it doesn't stick right away. Keep showing up, keep putting in the reps, and trust that the compound effect will work its magic.

Remember, changing your habits is not about perfection, it's about progress. It's about becoming the kind of person who does the things that align with the life you want to live. That kind of transformation doesn't happen overnight.

If you stay committed, if you keep showing up and doing the work even when it's hard, even when you don't feel like it, you will change. Your habits will change. And your life will change as a result.

So take a deep breath, pick a habit, and get started. Your redefined life is waiting for you, one tiny habit at a time.

STEP FIVE: BE RESILIENT

Alright, you've gotten fed up, gotten clear, made a plan, and started changing your habits. You're on the path to redefining your life but here's the thing—the path is not going to be smooth. There will be obstacles, setbacks, and challenges that will make you want to quit. There will be days or weeks or months where you feel like you're taking two steps forward and three steps back.

That's where resilience comes in. Resilience is the ability to bounce back from adversity, to keep going even when shit gets hard, to fall down seven times and stand up eight. If you want to redefine your life, you've got to cultivate resilience like it's your fucking job.

Here's the truth: Life is not going to go according to plan. You will face rejections, failures, and disappointments. You will have days where you don't believe in yourself, where you question everything, where you want to give up. In those moments, your resilience will be the thing that keeps you going. So how do you become resilient? It's time to train your mind and your heart to weather the storms.

YOUR ACTION ITEMS:

1. Reframe failure. Failure is not the opposite of success, it's a part of success. Every successful person has failed, often many times. The difference is they don't let failure define them. They see it as a learning opportunity, a chance to grow and improve. When you face a setback, ask yourself: What can I learn from this? How can I use this to become better, stronger, wiser?
2. Practice self-compassion. You are going to fuck up. You are going to have days where you don't show up as your best

THE REDEFINING PROCESS

self. When that happens, you have a choice: You can beat yourself up, or you can treat yourself with kindness and understanding. Choose the latter. Talk to yourself like you would talk to a beloved friend who's going through a hard time. Be gentle, be supportive, be encouraging. Resilience is not about being perfect, it's about being kind to yourself when you're not.

3. Find your why. When the going gets tough, you need a reason to keep going. You need a why that's bigger than your momentary discomfort. Get clear on your why. Why are you doing this? What's at stake? What will happen if you give up? What kind of life are you fighting for? Write it down, say it out loud, tattoo it on your heart. Let your why be the anchor that keeps you grounded when the storms come.
4. Build your support system. No one is an island, and no one achieves anything great alone. You need people in your corner who believe in you, who support you, who will pick you up when you fall down. Build your tribe. Find your mentors, your cheerleaders, your accountability partners. Surround yourself with people who lift you up, who inspire you, who challenge you to be your best self.
5. Take care of yourself. Resilience is not about pushing yourself to the brink of exhaustion. It's about taking care of yourself so you have the energy and the stamina to keep going. Prioritize self-care. Get enough sleep, eat nourishing foods, move your body, take breaks when you need them. Treat yourself like the precious, valuable, amazing human being that you are.

Remember that resilience is not a destination, it's a practice. It's something you cultivate day by day, moment by moment. The more you practice, the stronger you'll become. So when the setbacks come (and they will), when the doubts creep in (and they will), when you want to give up (and you will), remember this: You are resilient. You have what it takes to weather any storm, to overcome any obstacle, to redefine your life on your own terms.

Take a deep breath, put on your big-kid pants, and keep fucking going. Your redefined life is waiting for you, and it's going to take every ounce of resilience you've got to claim it. But you've got this. I believe in you. More importantly, you've got to believe in yourself.

There is one caveat to staying focused and being relentless with your goals, and that is to know when your plan isn't working. If you've stayed focused, followed the steps, and you're not seeing the results because your behavior isn't changing, you may need a new plan. Don't be unwilling to modify your original plan if it isn't yielding results. You may have to tweak it. You may have to throw it in the trash and start a new one. Evaluate and shift when and where necessary.

Start today. This is not one of those five-year plans. Whatever you decide to do, put it in motion *today*. Start now.

What are you waiting for?

KEEP REDEFINING

You did it!. You committed to this process, and you're making radical changes in your life. To get to this point, you had to choose yourself. For once, you put your own needs ahead of everyone else's, understanding that when you win, so does everyone around you. For that reason alone, you should be fucking proud.

If you take nothing else away from this book, I want you to:

- See yourself as someone who can do whatever the hell you set your mind to.
- Realize that you have the power to change your life whenever you damn well please.

THE REDEFINING PROCESS

- Know that you deserve a great life, no matter what anyone else says.
- Remember, you can define yourself–and redefine–over and over again.

I packed a nice and neat process into this book, and being the no-bullshit coach that I am, I wanted to make changing your life as straightforward as possible. If you commit to this work, you will see results. I guaran-fucking-tee it.

But let's keep it real: Redefining yourself is a journey, not a destination. It's not a one-and-done kind of deal. It's a lifelong process of unlearning and relearning, of shedding old skin and growing new layers. That's okay, that's how it should be.

Think of it like a snake shedding its skin. Stay with me, I promise this metaphor is going somewhere. A snake doesn't just shed its skin once and then coast for the rest of its life. It keeps shedding, keeps growing, keeps transforming. Each time it emerges, it's a little bit stronger, a little bit wiser, a little bit more badass.

That's you, you magnificent snake. (I mean that in the best possible way.) Every time you redefine yourself, every time you shed an old layer and step into a new one, you're becoming more of who you were meant to be.

So don't stop. Keep shedding. Keep growing. Keep redefining. Even when it's uncomfortable, even when it's scary, even when you feel like you're crawling out of your own skin–which, let's be real, you kind of are. Trust the process. Trust yourself.

When you need a reminder of how far you've come and how much further you can go, come back to this book. Revisit the exercises. Reread the stories. Reconnect with the fire that brought you here in the first place.

Most of all, keep putting in the work. Keep showing up for yourself. Keep believing that you are worth the effort, the discomfort, the growth because you are. You always have been.

When you look in the mirror, I want you to see the person you've always known you could be. The person without limits. The person who isn't weighed down by anyone else's bullshit expectations or judgments. The person who is free to be, do, and have whatever the fuck they want.

The person who decided to redefine—and never stopped.

Now I'm passing the torch to you. It's your turn to take this process and make it your own. Your turn to keep redefining yourself, in your own way, on your own terms.

So here's my challenge to you: Take one bold, audacious, scary-as-fuck step toward your next level of redefinition. Do something that makes you uncomfortable. Have a conversation that scares the shit out of you. Make a move that feels like jumping off a cliff (metaphorically, please—no actual cliff-jumping necessary).

When you've done that, come tell me about it in our Facebook group https://www.facebook.com/groups/1659288621491352/ or email me at lhayes@strategicbehaviorconsutants.com. Share your story with me, with this community, with the world because your story matters. Your redefinition matters. And you never know who you might inspire to start redefining themselves just by being brave enough to share your own journey.

So go forth! Keep growing. Keep redefining, and know that I'm in your fucking corner, cheering you on every step of the way.

Let's show the world what it looks like to live a life that's authentic, unapologetic, and truly fucking redefined.

CONCLUSION

We've come to the end of this wild ride together but let's be real, this isn't an ending. It's a beginning. The beginning of your new life as a redefined badass.

Throughout this book, we've covered some serious ground. We've dug into the shit that's been holding you back—the limiting beliefs, the self-sabotage, the fear of change. We've called out the bullshit excuses and the tired-ass stories you've been telling yourself. I've given you the tools and the mindset shifts you need to start redefining yourself on your own terms.

But here's the thing: All the knowledge in the world won't do shit if you don't apply it. If you don't take action. If you don't do the fucking work.

So that's my final challenge to you: Don't let this book be just another thing you read and forget about. Don't let the fire that's been lit inside you flicker out. Don't let yourself slide back into old patterns and habits just because they're comfortable.

Instead, take what you've learned here and run with it. Put it into practice every damn day. Keep pushing yourself out of your comfort zone. Keep shedding old layers and growing new ones. Keep redefining what's possible for your life.

When shit gets hard (because it will), when you want to give up (because you will), come back to this book. Come back to this community. Come back to the truth of who you are and what you're capable of.

Here's what I know for sure: You are a fucking force to be reckoned with. You have the power to create a life that sets your soul on fire. You have the power to redefine yourself again and again in the face of whatever challenges come your way.

But you have to choose it. You have to claim it. You have to fight for it, every day.

Let this book be your battle cry. Let it be your roadmap. Let it be your reminder of what you're made of and what you're here to do.

And let it be the spark that ignites a revolution, not just in your own life but in the lives of every person you touch. Because when you redefine yourself, you give others permission to do the same. We become a walking, talking, living, breathing example of what's possible when we have the courage to shed our old stories and step into our power.

So go out there and live your truth. Be your own kind of beautiful. And never, ever stop redefining what's possible.

I believe in you. I'm proud of you. I can't wait to see the magic you create.

Here's to your redefinition and to a life that's wilder, freer, and more authentic than your wildest dreams.

ABOUT THE AUTHOR

LaKeysha Cobbs-Hayes, MAT, BCBA, is a force of nature. Born into a world that told her who she could be, LaKeysha defied every limitation placed upon her. Surviving sexual abuse, abandonment, and the foster care system, she refused to let her circumstances define her destiny.

Against all odds, LaKeysha transformed her life. From a high school graduate with all Ds to a master's degree holder, from a teen mom to CEO of the multi-million dollar behavioral health company Key Essentials to Behavior Management Corp., and Strategic Behavior Consultants, LaKeysha rewrote her story and redefined what was possible.

Today, LaKeysha is on a mission to empower others to do the same. As a behavior analyst, behavior mindset coach, and speaker, she shares her hard-won wisdom and practical strategies for overcoming adversity, building resilience, and creating a life on your own terms.

LaKeysha's influence extends beyond her professional achievements. She is a devoted wife of more than 20 years, a mother of six, and a proud grandmother. She cherishes her roles at home as much as her roles in the boardroom and on stage.

Redefined is LaKeysha's rallying cry for anyone who has ever been told they can't. With her trademark blend of expert insight, down-to-earth wisdom, and infectious enthusiasm, LaKeysha is here to help you shed your past, own your present, and redefine your future.

Are you ready to redefine what's possible? LaKeysha is living proof that you can. For more information, visit www.lakeyshacobbshayes.com.

www.ingramcontent.com/pod-product-compliance
Lightning Source LLC
Chambersburg PA
CBHW052142070526
44585CB00017B/1938